AF422102

*Tapestry Threads:*
*Life, Death, & Resilience*

Also by Ashley M. Stephenson

*Rise Up: Be Resilient Like You're Running Out of Time*

# Tapestry Threads:
# Life, Death, & Resilience

Ashley M. Stephenson

Time to Rise Press, LLC values and supports copyright. Copyright fuels creativity, encourages diverse voices, promotes free speech, and creates a vibrant culture. Please note that no part of this book may be used or reproduced in any matter for the purpose of training artificial intelligence technologies or systems.

Disclaimer: This book is intended to provide information and inspiration related to the topics discussed. By its publication and sale, neither the author nor the publisher is engaged in rendering psychological, therapeutic, or other professional services. If you are in need of mental health or psychological assistance, please seek the services of a qualified professional.

The views and opinions expressed in this book are those of the author alone and do not necessarily reflect those of any organizations, institutions, or individuals with whom the author may be affiliated, unless explicitly stated. The author's intent is not to malign any group, organization, company, individual, or religion.

---

**Copyright © 2026 by Time to Rise Press, LLC**
ISBN (Paperback): 979-8-9935201-0-0
ISBN (Ebook): 979-8-9935201-1-7
Library of Congress Control Number: 2026906048

All rights reserved.
Published in the United States.
First Edition.

*For those who stood in the fray and called it fabric.*

# CONTENTS

# PROLOGUE

In the quiet whispers of yesterday's light,
the only way forward is through the past.
For wisdom blooms where memories reside —
I write what I know; time moves too fast.

Each tale I carry, a tapestry true,
threads intertwine — old and new.
No longer mine alone to bear,
but shared with hearts beyond compare.

Let us embrace the tales we've spun,
in every verse, our spirits run.
For in our stories, we are one —
a testament to what we've become.

With pen in hand, through joy and pain,
we write, we lose, we love, we gain.
The stories we tell forever endure,
guiding us onward — stronger, pure.

May these words be balm to the soul,
mending the broken, making whole.
In every thread of grief and grace,
find healing — and your sacred place.

With woven words of hope and resilience,

*Ashley M. Stephenson*

# LIFE

*The pulse of beginnings.*
*Of sunlight and shadow interwoven.*
*Of choices that shape and moments that scan —*
*And still, the heart beats on.*

# Golden Hues of Yesterday

Take me back to the days when life wasn't heavy,
to moments so light, our hearts ready to levitate.
When the sunlight danced through leaves so cheery,
and time was a friend, not a pending due date.

Remember the laughter that bubbled from deep,
the careless whispers in the dead of the night,
when secrets were sacred, left for our keep,
and every small hill seemed a mountain of might.

We chased after dreams with fervent abandon,
in a world so vast, yet felt so small.
Where the promise of morning was our only canon,
and every leap of faith, a thrilling call.

Take me back to those days of simplistic pleasure,
when every raindrop was a melody,
and the cosmos itself seemed to treasure,
our youthful zeal, our untamed glee.

Let's find that path, hidden and forgotten,
beneath layers of life's relentless fray.
To those days when life wasn't heavy,
and bask once more in the dawn of an unburdened day.

Take me back to those golden hues, when smiles were freely given,
to those untouched fields where we roamed beneath the vast, open
heaven.
Where the air was sweeter and filled with the scent of hope,
and the horizon was a canvas for our dreams' broad scope.

Let's return to the nights under the stars' watchful eyes,
where the only limit was the universe's size.
We laid on the ground, making wishes on shooting stars,
believing in magic, that nothing felt too far.

Recall the spontaneous journeys, no destination in mind,
every turn on the road, a new wonder we'd find.
Life was an adventure, waiting just outside our door,
every moment rich, promising so much more.

To the first sip of freedom, so intoxicating and new,
where every experience added a different hue.
Our spirits were unbridled, wild horses running free,
in an endless meadow, our playground to be.

Bring me back to the threshold of dawn and dusk,
when the colors of the sky were a painter's brush.
In that soft light, all worries seemed to fade,
in the embrace of twilight, all debts were paid.

Let's unearth that innocence, once known and lived,
before the world taught us to take more than we give.
To the days when life wasn't heavy, but a breeze
caressing our faces, setting our minds at ease.

May we wander back, even just in our heart's reverie,
to those days of pure joy, where our souls were truly free,
and maybe, just maybe, in remembering, we'll
a trace of that peace, left behind.

# Stitches of Strength

In the backseat —
a sudden boom, chaos unfurls,
a glimpse of a blue shirt,
covered in blood and curls.

Confusion sets in,
pain coursing through veins,
fear gripping so tight —
a touch of the cheek, stains.
Hand covered in blood,
the world fading from sight.

A blood-and-tear-stained face
lying on the sidewalk,
a stranger rushing inside,
compassion in full force,
with hard brown paper towels,
trying to halt life's remorse.

Thoughts of dying,
soul filled with dread,
but paramedics arrived —
rescue threads spread.

Through the emergency room,
hopes intertwine,
thirty stitches sewn,
marking scars that redefine.

Scars on one side of the face,
a reflection forever changed —
yet he, the cause of this pain,
walked away, not suffering the same.

Resilience—
who would have thought
was being formed then,

in the crucible of despair?
Little did she know,
its impact would be everywhere.

From that harrowing moment,
strength began to take root.
Her spirit bloomed
with a newfound will,
steadfast and resolute.
The scars on her face —
a testament to survival's song,
a reminder that resilience
can triumph over every wrong.

Twenty-three years later,
she stood in that exact same spot.
Memories replay —
the pain endured never forgot.

Where she laid,
blood rushing down her face,
for years she prayed
he too would suffer in this place.

Embracing memories,
the pain she has endured,
shaping her into someone
resilient and assured.

Life's dance continues,
forcing her to wear
her scars with pride —
for they remind her
that from darkness,
we can always rise.

# Discomfort as Fuel

In finding your passion, you follow your fear,
embracing the unknown, making intentions clear.
From small-town dreams to Manhattan's bright gleam,
you dare to chase life, a vivid, bold dream.

Comfort in discomfort — the heart of evolution,
in uneasy moments, we find resolution.
Growth whispers softly through trials unknown,
in facing the challenge, our true selves are shown.

Venture forth boldly along winding ways,
let fear guide your steps through uncertain days.
In discomfort's embrace, we find strength and light,
our journey unfolding, a flight into height.

Beneath city skies, where skyscrapers rise,
dreamers and doers reach for the skies.
Doubt once lingered, now confidence strong,
embracing the challenge, where hearts belong.

Ambition ignites, setting fire to the soul,
in pursuit of dreams, achieving each goal.
Stepping from comfort into the unknown,
discovering new depths in places unshown.

Hearts beating courageous, passion afire,
breaking through barriers, climbing higher and higher.
The road may be rocky, the path may be steep,
but in discomfort, we find the dreams we keep.

Embrace the fear — let it fuel your **flame,**
for in discomfort's grip, you'll claim your name.
A journey of growth, unfolding each day,
in courage and challenge, we find our own way.

# Ties That Bond

In the twilight of a cherished connection,
a story unfolds of closeness and disconnection,
I remember the vibrant moments we shared,
threads of resilience proving we cared.

I watched you laugh, consumed by pure delight,
yet from a distance, I kept out of sight,
A flicker of envy stirred in my eye,
longing to join you, to share the same scene.

But doubts lingered in my hesitant heart,
fearful of rejection, of being torn apart.
So I built quiet walls of caution and guise,
unaware that strength could help me rise.

Amid the chatter and laughter all around,
you moved closer, your presence profound.
No greetings exchanged, no words were said,
yet your quiet attention lingered, softly spread.

In that moment, a glimmer pierced my core,
realizing friendship comes with a price to explore,
For in life's grand theater with all its scenes,
resilience guides us toward our dreams.

Rewind to the coffee shops on Conn. Avenue,
nothing ventured, nothing gained — we lamented,
Phone calls and invitations, an unending loop,
eventually, we chose another path, a different group.

As time moves on, our paths diverged,
yet memories of our closeness still emerge,
And through this journey, I've come to see,
that resilience is the key to setting our hearts free.

So I bid farewell to a once-cherished bond,
knowing that resilience will help me respond,
To new beginnings where friendships will grow,
with strength and courage, embracing the unknown.

Through the scattered leaves of seasons gone by,
we carry the warmth of moments that won't die,
Resilience blooms where old bonds once lay,
guiding our steps into each new day.

# Clandestine Operations

You wiped away the mascara from my tear-stained face,
a fleeting moment of sweet ephemera,
I can unravel around you, though I don't know why —
kindred spirits, you whispered in the night,
our connection shining bright.

Feelings kept hidden,
a secret rendezvous,
like that night we talked for hours
and you called back just to say *"I love you."*

In the stillness of the night, a gentle voice,
saying the words that eased my mind,
solace found amidst the pain.
Navigating feelings, pleasure, and strain.

Complications arise,
creating a web of deceit,
yet in your presence,
my heart finds retreat.

Brooklyn nights filled with whispered words,
a connection like no other, deeply stirred.
Tears wiped away, mascara stains fade,
kindred spirits in a quiet serenade.

A moment imprinted, forever marked,
in a New York minute, our fates embarked.
Concealed emotions, secrets interlace,
in your arms, a peaceful place.

Embarking on a fresh journey,
uncovering hidden truths we seek,
your touch, a balm that soothes,
bringing comfort to the weak.

Entwined like kindred spirits,
tethered by threads unseen,
engaged in this clandestine operation,
transforming our daily scene.

In the quiet of the night, shadows play,
echoes of memories set adrift and stray.
Whispers of love, a symphony of grace,
embracing in the darkness, finding our place.
Entwined by struggles and shared fate,
an eternal bond that will not dissipate.
In the city that never sleeps,
promises made and secrets guarded deep,
vulnerability intertwined yet secure in place.

Brooklyn bridges connecting our souls,
a tapestry of stories, untold roles.
Laughter and tears, woven in song,
in each other's presence, we belong.

A moment fleeting, an enduring glow,
spirits entwined in a gentle light.
Unspoken truths, beneath the disguise,
in the tapestry of love, where our essence lies.

In your touch, solace unfolds,
in the quiet echoes, promises mold.
Kindred spirits in a world unknown,
love blossoms where shadows have grown.

# Bittersweet Refrain

In the depths of confusion, yet certain of your allure,
half-spoken words, carried a truth obscure.
Always drawn to your essence from afar,
in love with the soul you are.

Beneath the surface, drowning in despair,
on bended knee, tears in the air.
Truth and lies entwined in a tangled lore,
you wanted me, but loved the bottle more.

A dance of dependency, toxic and unkind,
as I sought to break free, leaving you behind.
You knew my soul, my quirks, my fears,
healing wounds that had lingered for years.

In hindsight, roles shifted, stark and clear,
you descending, as I rose from the dark.
Memories now drift like a distant stream,
before the anger, before the shattered dream.

Passion ablaze, emotions raw and untamed,
fierce battles waged, no victory named.
Consumed by love, flames too intense to touch,
perhaps in loving, we loved too much.

Closure elusive, an unspoken end,
amidst chaos and broken pieces we mend.
Unplanned twists, hopes reduced to dust,
the foundation crumbles, turning to rust.

My mind recalls the dance in the gloom,
in the forest of our love, a wilted bloom.
No need for words, just music's gentle hum,
yet destiny, in its silence, strikes numb.

Reflections in the mirror, no longer the same,
a shattered image, bearing the blame.

The echo of what was, now fades in the gloom,
leaving behind a bittersweet tune.

In the tapestry of time, our story woven deep,
moments of ecstasy, sorrow, and sleep.
Threads of passion intertwined with doubt,
tangled emotions we couldn't live without.
Silent whispers in the night, hauntingly clear,
echoes of the past drawing near.
Promises broken, dreams left to rust,
love lost and crumbled to dust.

Yet in the wreckage, a glimmer of light,
a chance for healing, for things set right.
Lessons learned, scars to prove,
the beauty of love, the pain it behooves.

As the sun sets on our twisted tale,
new beginnings rise from the stale.
Embracing the change, the unknown ahead,
in the aftermath of what we once bled.

So we part ways, hearts heavy yet free,
a shared journey, now a memory.
Through the chaos, the tears, and the gloom,
a bittersweet tune echoes through the room.

# Canvas of Moments

In the grand tapestry of life we're wove,
threads of joy and pain in patterns strove.
Moments of laughter, moments of tears,
we navigate the passage of years.

Through winding paths, we chase the sun,
triumphs and trials, each story spun.
Shaping our journey, stirring the heart,
every ending opens a brand-new start.

In the stillness of night, the chaos of day,
we seek meaning along the way.
Through love and loss, we rise and grow,
embracing the highs, enduring the low.

Life's canvas painted in shades profound,
each stroke a tale, each color unbound.
In unity and solitude, we find our peace,
an ever-evolving, wondrous masterpiece.

Savor each moment the present brings,
let go of shadows, let your spirit sing.
For in the end, it's the memories made,
that define our essence, never to fade.

May we dance in fields of blooming grace,
meet challenges boldly, with courage and pace.
As time unfolds its intricate strands,
let us hold each other's hearts in our hands.

With every step, a story told,
every echo a saga bold.
Compose your melody, let it ring,
in harmony, let your spirit sing.

Embrace the journey, with love sincere,
no moment wasted, no memory unclear.
For when the final sun dips low,
our legacy will shine, a radiant glow.

# Solace Amidst Pain

In the depths of loneliness and despair,
a weight unseen hangs heavy in the air.
It strikes the heart, it twists the core,
leaving you staggering, locked behind the door.

A sharp ache in the chest, a knot in the core,
breathing becomes a battle, standing is a chore,
the weight of anguish, heavy and deep,
overwhelming emotions, hard to keep.

What kind of pain has touched your soul?
The kind that leaves you feeling less than whole,
tearing through you with relentless force,
leaving you gasping, staying on course.

May healing come, may peace find its way,
through the darkness, guiding the day,
remember, dear heart, you're not alone,
in the midst of pain, seeds of growth are sown.

As time passes, wounds may start to heal,
the pain less intense, less raw to feel,
but the scars remain, a reminder of the past,
a testament to the strength that will forever last.

Hold onto hope, let it be your guide,
through the valleys and peaks of this emotional ride,
for in the depths of loneliness and despair,
there's a silver lining, waiting to repair.

# Fragments of Memories

In the halls of memory, echoes softly weep,
of a love that once blossomed, now buried deep.
I sit and write of someone who used to be you,
how skies turned from bright to a muted hue.

In the quiet of the night, tears start to fall,
sobbing on the ground, heartbreak's bitter sound.
Mascara racing down, leaving stains of pain,
a kaleidoscope of emotions, dancing in the rain.

You spoke of shades beyond black and white,
yet dimmed the hues of my once-vivid sight.
Piece by piece, the color drained away,
leaving me lost in shadows of gray.

Dreams we shared now shattered like glass,
fragments of memories slipping past.
Whispers of laughter replaced by silence,
filling the air with a heavy absence.

I searched for answers in corridors of doubt,
lost in the maze of what love was about.
Yet amid the darkness, a flicker of light,
a promise of healing after the night.

But amidst the shadows, a flicker of light,
a promise of healing, of dawn after night.
A reminder that pain does not define,
that in time, a new chapter will shine.

Through the haze of sorrow, I find strength to rise,
ready to reclaim the colors that once painted my skies.
Though memories linger, with their bittersweet allure,
I'll paint a new canvas, brighter and pure.

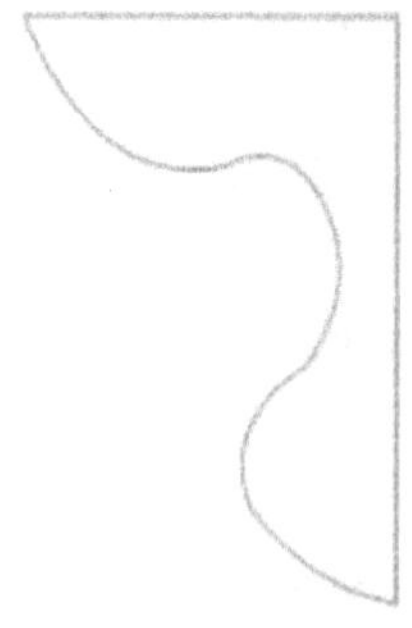

# Threads Unwoven

In this tapestry of life, we were once woven,
two souls tangled in vows we didn't know how to keep.
Now I stand surrounded by pieces
of promises that broke on contact.
It turns out
I don't even know you anymore.

That summer never asked permission.
Sorrento heat clung to our skin,
air thick with salt and laughter.
Mascara streaked down my face —
not from sadness, but from living too loudly.
You watched me fall apart
like it was proof I was real.

Even in my worst of times,
you could see the best of me.
Even when I was unsteady,
you swore I was solid ground.

My rebounds. My earthquakes.
The nights I lied to survive the mornings.
The truths I hid in jokes,
the fear I buried under motion.
And still
even in the lies,
you could see the truth in me.

You were my oath.
I was your secret.
We learned how to love in fragments,
how to keep something alive
by never saying its name out loud.

I thought I knew you —
or maybe I knew who you were
when loving me felt effortless.
Now your name feels unfamiliar,
a sound I practiced for years
without learning its meaning.

You think I'm bulletproof.
I'm not.
I fracture quietly,
splintering where no one looks.

Give me something that will haunt me
when you're not around —
something louder than this absence,
something heavier than silence.

Your touch is gone,
but it still echoes on my body.
We were a flight risk
with a fear of falling,
yet somehow I trusted the air
as long as it was you beneath me.

The verdict never came.
Only distance did.
Ghosts from your past kept calling you backward
while I stayed here,
learning how to stand
without shrinking myself to be chosen.

You memorized my every move —
or I believed you did.
All roads led me back to you
until one day
they didn't.

She asked me how I was doing.
I had no language for it.
How do you explain
that love doesn't end —
it fractures?

I wanted to be part of the narrative,
not just a chapter you abandoned mid-sentence.
Once, all I knew was you.
Once, you said you couldn't live without me.
And part of me hoped that was true.
Part of me still does,
and resents myself for believing.

Now there's nothing left to defend,
no vows to repair, no silence to decode.
Just the aftermath,
finally honest.
From the wreckage, I gather the threads.
Endings and beginnings blur when you're bleeding.
We don't rewrite what was
we stitch forward.

New seams.
A different pattern.
One that doesn't require disappearing
to be loved.

Time waits.
The canvas is clean.
And I step into what comes next
with hands empty,
ready to hold something
that stays.

# Shifting Tides of Life

Funny how things change, like the shifting of tides,
once on top of the world, with nothing left to hide.
Cheering one another on, through nights dark and days bright,
but tragedy struck quickly, altering our light.

All came to a halt, our unity torn asunder,
moving on in different directions,
yet respect and admiration linger, a flickering flame,
I miss seeing you around, in whispers of your name.

Time may pass, and distances stretch wide,
but the bond we once shared will quietly reside.
In life's vast tapestry, threads of memory intertwine,
and I hope you never forget moments that were mine.

Through the stormy seas of change, we sailed our separate ways,
but the memories we created still color my days.
I cherish the laughter, the tears that we shed,
and the unspoken words between us, left unsaid.

Life spins its web, weaving stories untold,
each chapter a thread, each memory a gold.
In the silence of absence, do echoes rise,
holding on tightly, through tear-blurred eyes.

Here's to the future, where paths may diverge,
yet the bond we forged continues to urge
us to remember the friendship we once knew,
In the changing tides of life, I carry it true.

# Blurred Lines

In a realm of shifting shadows and whispers,
where secrets dance with forbidden desires,
I wander through the labyrinth of deceit,
yearning for a glimpse of truth to meet.

Boundaries like delicate threads unwind,
as I navigate this dangerous path,
hiding from prying eyes and judgmental minds,
yet drawn to the thrill of the aftermath that follows.

*"You blur the lines, yet expect me to see the boundary,"*
as I teeter on the edge of what's forbidden,
my heart races, my resolve overridden.

Lost in the tangled maze of deceit,
I search for a flicker of honesty,
but the lines blur further, the risk entwined,
in the web of secrets so clandestine.

Navigating this treacherous terrain,
I am both the hunter and the prey,
embracing the perilous allure
of a *"what if"* meant to be kept at bay.

For in the midst of this twisted dance,
I find a mirror reflecting my own essence,
embracing the chaos, the ecstasy,
of something that defies all preconceived notions.

In the dance of shadows, I am entwined,
between what's right and what's undefined,
a fragile balance on the edge of reason,
navigating through this treacherous season.

Each step I take, a risk so profound,
in the echo chamber of whispers around,
I embrace the mystery, the thrill of the chase,
lost in the whirlwind, caught in its embrace.

Like a moth drawn to a flickering flame,
I am lured by the allure, the forbidden game,
with every heartbeat, a whisper of deceit,
in this realm where truth and fiction meet.

Amidst the chaos, a revelation blooms,
a tapestry of secrets, a myriad of hints,
I surrender to the dance of shadows deep,
in this labyrinth where secrets forever keep.

# A Love Unraveled

In the midst of shadows deep and dim,
an affair entwined, once full of whim.
Did this love lose its spark, illicit no more?
Am I the Judas you shunned to the core?

Beneath the moon's betrayed light,
I ponder our story, a somber sight.
Time wasted. Hearts torn.
In this bitter truth, we're sadly worn.

Like a voice that breaks while trying to soar,
and sentences that wound long after the last word.
We danced in a tragedy, twisted and dark,
a love that left us with a lasting mark.

So good, yet so bad for my fragile heart.
A love that tears me apart.
I cry out in despair, longing for your touch,
hoping you'll pick me up before I'm crushed.

In the quiet echoes of the past,
our love, once vibrant, couldn't last.
Whispers of regrets linger on
in shadows where our hearts have gone.

Through the veil of time and space,
I search for a glimpse of your face.
Memories of laughter now stained with tears,
love lost in the passage of years.

A love entangled in secrets untold,
betrayal's bitter tale unfold.
In the garden where roses wither and wilt,
we buried our love, layer by layer, with guilt.

Waves of sorrow crash and break.
Dreams shattered. Hearts ache.

In the tapestry of our tangled fate,
threads of love and loss interweave, intricate.

In the solace of the moon's soft glow,
a restless heart beats, longing to know
if redemption's grace could find its way
to heal the wounds of yesterday.

Through the pages of our story untold,
echoes of love, once bold.
I stand in the shadows, consumed by pain,
hoping someday we'll dance in the light again.

# Chapters of You

In the chapters of your story, I find
a tale that lingers in heart and mind.
I return to your pages time and again,
savoring the words, their joy and pain.

I read it again and again,
each time discovering something new to mend.
The depth of emotions, the twists and bends,
every reading a journey that never descends.

Somehow the only thing that stays consistent is it ends.
A bittersweet truth as the plot transcends,
leaving me longing for what could have been,
but grateful for the memories it tends.

Although there's not many pages,
there are so many details, down through the ages.
Each word a brushstroke on life's endless canvas,
painting a picture that forever engages.

So I'll revisit your chapter, over and over again,
finding solace in the prose that does not wane.
For in the story of you, I find my refrain,
a symphony of moments, a beautiful strain.

Through the valleys and peaks, the love and pain,
your story shines bright, in sunshine or rain.
And as I turn each page with a pang of disdain,
I realize that in your tale, there's so much to gain.

In every scene, a treasure to find,
in every line, a message that's kind.
Your words, like a gentle wind that's benign,
guiding me through the maze of your magnificent design.

And when the final chapter does arrive,
I'll hold onto the memories and strive
to carry them forward, keep them alive,
in my heart where your story will forever thrive.

# Champagne & Shadows

For those who can relate
to crying with a celebratory glass of champagne nearby,
wishful shadows of what could have been
silently unravel.

There's a world where I call
and update you on my life's course,
but the conversation tends to leave me feeling worse —
a mix of bittersweetness, a longing, a curse.

I imagine you listening
perhaps smiling, perhaps distracted
and still the ache remains,
a bittersweet reminder
that some bridges cannot be crossed.

Another world reveals
where achievements rise, dreams take flight,
where city lights echo my small-town ambitions,
you always said I'd make a name for myself,
and yet your absence dims the light.

In the midst of these parallel worlds,
I search for solace, for a bridge to collide,
a way to reconcile the pain and the pride,
to find a balance where joy and sadness coincide.

For those who can relate to these intricate ties,
of celebrating with tears and silent sighs,
may we find peace in the worlds we inhabit,
as we hold onto memories, cherishing every bit.

For it is through pain and triumph we grow,
our resilience quietly aglow,
and in our hearts, love still shines bright,
even across absence and night.

# Forever Enshrined

In the depths of my heart, his presence lingers,
a love enduring, memory's soft fingers.
Forever entwined through the tides of time,
his essence remains, quietly sublime.

His laughter echoes, his touch still near,
in corridors of thought, his spirit clear.
Understanding my fears, embracing my flaws,
in his arms I found solace, without pause.

Together we danced, a waltz of fate,
life's symphony playing, harmonious, innate.
Hand in hand, we faced the storms,
bound by a love that kept us warm.

But tides turned bitter, winds blew cold,
struggles emerged, tears uncontrolled.
Yet amid the chaos, a glimmer shone,
love's ember endured, never gone.

Time's sands relentless, sweeping dreams away,
yet in the ruins, our love still stays.
Though roads diverged and destinies part,
he remains a beacon within my heart.

I'll cherish the memories, hold them dear,
for in my mind, his presence is always near.
A love transcending time and space,
a bittersweet symphony, tender, laced.

# Emotions Unmasked

In the world of masks and hidden truths,
I see the smile that often soothes.
But behind those eyes, a shadow lies,
a hidden sadness that defies.

Intrigued by the smile on one's face,
and the sadness within their eyes, a quiet space.
Despite the words shared or penned,
Some feelings in the heart are too vast to comprehend.

There's a depth within, a silent cry,
A feeling too heavy to express, too high to fly.
So we carry on, with our masks in place,
Hiding the turmoil in our heart's secret space.

But let us remember, beneath the disguise,
We all hold emotions, both lows and highs.
Seek to understand, offer a listening ear,
For within each of us, there's a story so dear.

In the tapestry of life's intricate design,
We encounter moments that intertwine.
Threads of joy and sorrow weave,
Creating a story that can help set one free.

Each soul carries a burden, unseen,
A mix of memories, both bright and keen.
Through laughter and tears, we find our way,
Navigating the ebb and flow of each day.

Let us be kind, tender-hearted, and true,
For we're all travelers in this journey too.
Peel back the layers, look beyond the guise,
And you'll discover beauty in the tears that arise.

Together we walk in this maze of life,
Amidst joy and pain, peace and strife.

Let us hold each other with gentle grace,
And embrace the complexities we face.

For within our hearts, a world resides,
Where emotions flow like changing tides.
In understanding and empathy, we find release,
And along the way, we discover lasting peace.

# Embracing Life's Symphony

In life's complex maze, we often tread,
between the good and the dread.
Like a ship sailing on uncertain sea,
navigating through highs and lows we see.

Life's melodies are twisted and sweet,
A symphony of trials where hearts still beat.
Each note a test, each chord a quest,
but in each crescendo, we find our best.

The dance of light and dark in play,
where shadows linger and sunbeams stray.
We seek balance in the murky haze,
carving our paths through winding ways.

I'm no Nietzsche, but I know it's true,
that good and bad exist, not just a few.
We tend to believe we're immune to the sorrow,
until it strikes, leaving us feeling hollow.

Yet in the heart of turmoil, seeds of hope,
root deep within, helping us cope.
We blossom in adversity's call,
rising unbroken, standing tall.

When troubles come, we fear we'll drown,
in despair and sorrows that weigh us down,
yet as days turn to weeks and years,
we find strength within, conquering fears.

Through the mists of time, we learn to see,
the tapestry of our journey, bold and free.
Each thread a story, woven with care,
in every setback, a lesson to bear.

Looking back, we see how far we've come,
through trials and tribulations, we've overcome.
"*I got through that,*" we say with pride,
for in every storm, we found a way to ride.

Remember in moments of strife,
the resilience within, the strength of life.
For when the shadows of doubt may ensue,
know that you have what it takes to pull through.

In the grand theater of life's grand design,
we play our parts, no matter the sign.
Remember, dear friend, you're never alone,
in this vast symphony, you have grown.

Embrace the journey, embrace the fight,
for in the darkest hour, shines the brightest light.
Keep sailing on the uncertain sea,
for in the waves, you'll find the key.

The key to unlock your inner might,
to conquer the darkness, to embrace the light.
So fear not the twists, fear not the turn,
for in the end, it's the lessons we learn.

And when the final curtain falls,
stand proud, heart ablaze through it all.
Having weathered life's tempestuous spree,
you shine, resilient, forever free.

# Firefly Whispers

In our youth, we chased fireflies so bright,
their gleaming lights illuminated the night.
Bold and joyous, eyes wide with wonder,
trailing their glow, laughing beneath the dark's cover.

Each flicker a star in our young eyes,
dancing across enchanted skies.
Through forests and fields, we'd roam,
following sparks that led us home.

Laughter and games lit our way,
spellbound by their luminous display.
Shadows and gleams learned how to dance,
guiding our hearts through childhood's trance.

As youths, we flew with spirits on high,
embracing the soft and gentle night sky.
Each flicker and gleam, our souls did ignite,
in this enchanting pursuit under the moonlight.

Time moves on, and fears take place,
yet deep within, their glow remains.
A spark of joy we cannot lose,
a whisper of innocence we still carry, not choose.

In midnight's embrace, solace appears,
recalling bright and carefree years.
Beneath the moon's silver gaze,
we remember the magic we were once brave enough to believe.

The fireflies' dance, a cherished memory's call,
trailing light across night's sprawl.
They lead us back to simpler times,
when wonder reigned and life spoke in rhymes.

So when the night feels heavy and vast,
seek the glow of a moment that will last.
For fireflies carry what time can't erase —
a lantern of wonder, a child's embrace.

# Inner Child

Beneath the weight of years,
I feel you waiting,
a small hand pressed against the glass
of memory,
eyes wide with wonder,
heart unscarred by what would come.

You speak in whispers
that echo through corridors of thought,
*"Do you remember?"*
and I do —
the fields we ran through,
the skies we traced with careless fingers,
the quiet magic of believing
everything was possible.

Yet the world arrived,
with its rules and sharp edges,
and we tucked you away,
folded in the corners of our mind,
a fragile spark that refused to die.

I reach for you now,
thread by trembling thread,
pulling loose the tapestry
of who we've become,
unraveling the weight
so you might breathe again.

Together we walk through shadowed woods,
through storms and stillness alike,
each step a negotiation
between what was,
what is,
and what might still be.

You teach me how to see the light,
how to laugh without asking permission,
how to trace the edges of wonder
even where grief has left its mark.

We are stitched together,
small hand in grown hand,
past and present woven tight,
each scar a seam,
each memory a thread
in the fabric of our becoming.

And though the years have tempered us,
though joy has learned restraint,
your voice still rises,
clear as sunlight through leaves:
*"Remember who you were.
Remember who you are."*

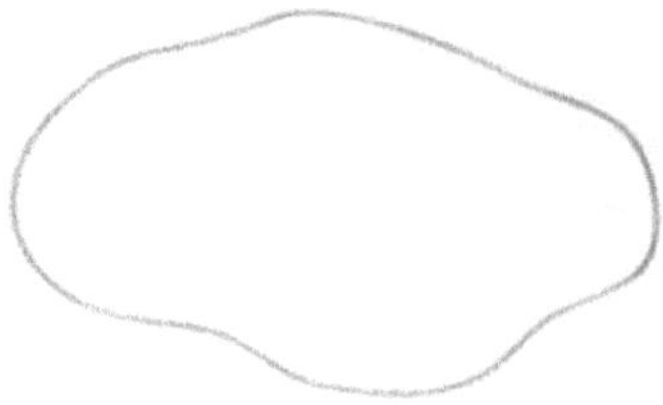

# Borrowed Time

Some moments arrive,
already ticking,
with laughter too bright,
and hands held too tight.

I knew even then
they were borrowed,
that joy sometimes comes
with a return label,
crease already folded,
address prewritten.

I pray to God He hears you,
and I pray He heals you,
because some hearts fracture inward,
and loving you meant listening
to damage I could never fix.

One question still haunts and hurts —
how do you save someone
who does not know
where they are bleeding?

Still, I spent them freely,
as if devotion could teach time mercy,
as if loving harder
might make the seconds hesitate,
might convince loss
to pass us by.

If time was going to take it back,
I wanted it warm,
worn in,
heavy with memory,
pressed into my hands
like proof.

Because borrowed does not mean empty,
and even what is taken
leaves an echo behind.

# Solace in Indifference

In the realm of emotions, I find solace in the unknown,
the place of indifference, better than the place of anger shown.
Where feelings wield their power, like waves crashing on the shore,
I choose a tranquil refuge, where peace forevermore.

Amidst the chaos, where voices clash and fray,
I stand unmoved, letting silence guide my way.
Here, in this calm, a sacred space unfolds,
a refuge for my spirit, a stillness to hold.

Let flames of rage fade, let storms dissolve to air,
I rest in quietude, free from worry or care.
In indifference, grace whispers soft and clear,
a gentle beacon, drawing my soul near.

In this sanctuary of stillness, I breathe in serenity,
unraveling the knots of worry with each exhale of clarity.
Embracing the whispers of calm, the echoes of peace,
finding solace in the quiet, where anxiety finds release.

Each breath untangles knots of restless thought,
revealing peace in moments once overwrought.
In the shadows of detachment, a light begins to gleam,
illuminating paths where I can dream.

Through the tide of life, unpredictable and vast,
I find my anchor, tethered to the calm that lasts.
Every sigh of acceptance lifts a burden away,
leaving space for joy to bloom, day by day.

Here I dwell, serene and whole,
a quiet witness to life's ebbing scroll.
No storm can reach this gentle place,
for I have found my solace in indifference's embrace.

# Embracing the Unknown

In a world where uncertainties abound,
Being content with what may come around,
If it happens or doesn't, in that space we find,
A place of strength, a tranquil mind.

Bones are the backbone of our frame,
Solid, sturdy, holding life's flame,
The rest, mere trinkets, passing chatter,
In the grand scheme, they hardly matter.

So let go of worry, embrace the unknown,
In our acceptance, our true selves are shown,
For in being okay with what fate presents,
We discover peace, in silence and in presence.

In this labyrinth of life's mysterious ways,
We navigate through the ebbs and flows of days,
Embracing the chaos, the twists, the turns,
As we dance with time, our hearts ever yearn.

The stars above, they twinkle and shine,
Guiding us through every mountain we climb,
With each step we take, a story is spun,
Threads of fate weaving, in the light of the sun.

Like branches reaching for the sky so high,
We too aim to soar, to spread our wings and fly,
Yet rooted we remain, grounded in our core,
Drawing strength from our past, forevermore.

Let the winds of change embrace our souls,
Into the unknown, we bravely stroll,
For in uncertainty lies endless possibility,
A canvas of dreams waiting to set us free.

Raise a glass to the unknown ahead,
A symphony of moments, woven thread by thread,
In surrendering to life's infinite dance,
We find beauty in every fleeting chance.

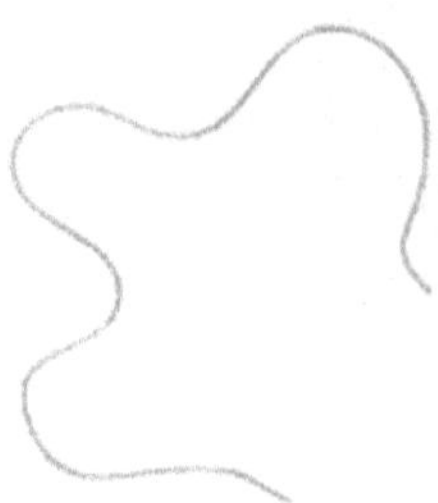

# Echoes of the Living Earth

You walk with boots that crush the ground beneath,
eyes set on gold, blind to the breath of leaves.
You claim the sky, the rivers, and the trees —
but do you feel the heartbeat in the breeze?

You measure worth in fences, flags, and stone,
yet leave the wildest wonders still unknown.
The soil you step on hums with ancient song,
and you, who think you lead, have listened wrong.

Have you ever let the starlight guide your name,
or danced beneath the thunder's silver flame?
Can you hear the silent stories in the rain,
or speak the language spoken by the crane?

Come walk the woven roots of whispering pine,
and sip the nectar sweetened by the vine.
Let go the hunger built by taking more —
and find the wealth not sold within a store.

The wolf and willow hold their sacred place,
not just for use, but beauty, truth, and grace.
The stream and sky, the hawk and trembling fawn,
are threads within the world we all live on.

You ask how tall a forest dream can grow,
but cut it down before you'll ever know.
And still you wonder why the songs don't last,
why echoes fade and future mirrors past.

For we are not apart — we are the thread,
alive within the living and the dead.
Until you feel the wind not as a foe,
but as a voice that teaches you to grow.

You'll walk this earth with empty hands and pride,
while all the colors bloom just out of sight.

# The Path I Paved

When I left town, did you hate me,
for abandoning the streets that raised me?
Did you curse my name as I packed my bags,
and headed off to explore new lands?

I couldn't help but feel the need to roam,
to see the world beyond my childhood home,
to find my place in something grander,
a purpose that my soul could anchor.

Each mile I put between us, I knew,
brought longing and guilt, and a sorrowful hue.
The eyes of those I loved still stayed,
haunted by moments we'd never replayed.

Settling into new lands, my heart still ached,
yet I trusted the choice I alone had made.
For chasing my dreams and carving my way,
I honored the path I chose that day.

Through cities vast and mountains high,
through plains where horizons stretch to the sky,
I met new faces, their stories untold,
each one a treasure, each encounter gold.

Yet deep inside, a familiar call,
the laughter and love I left in it all.
The echoes of youth, warm and bright,
guided me gently through the night.

So if leaving hurt, I hope you'll see,
the journey I took was meant to set me free.
And in the tale I continue to weave,
I honor the life I dared to believe.

# Memory Lane

If memory lane were a real place,
cobblestone paths laid in gentle grace,
each step would carry us back in time,
to moments of joy, to laughter sublime.

We'd stroll through gardens of forgotten dreams,
where laughter and love still flow in streams,
retracing the footsteps of days gone by,
beneath a soft and nostalgic sky.

Along the winding path of memory lane,
shadows linger where sunlight once danced,
each step echoes with laughter and sighs,
ghosts of yesterday held in the hush of leaves.

Time drifts like smoke through the hollow of trees,
curling around moments, fragile and bright,
the scent of old roses filling the air,
whispering stories we still hold dear.

Faces emerge in the mist of recollection,
their eyes soft lanterns guiding us home,
we touch the corners of old streets,
tracing the pulse of life we thought we knew.

Memory is a mirror, cracked yet clear,
reflecting who we were and who we might have been,
a tapestry woven in colors once bright,
where echoes of joy and sorrow intertwine.

I walk along memory lane,
where shadows linger softly,
and the air hums with whispers
of laughter, of tears, of long-forgotten light.

I pass familiar corners,
smelling rain on old pavements,
touching fences that held our stories,
windows catching the last glint of youth.

Time folds over itself here,
blurring edges, softening corners,
revealing how love and loss
are stitched into the seams of who we are.
And yet we walk, step by measured step,
through the haze of blue and gray,
learning that memory is both burden and balm,
both the weight we carry and the wings we grow.

If memory lane were a real place,
I would linger there a little longer,
each whisper clear, each moment treasured,
carrying the past forward like a lantern,
lighting the way home.

# Emerald Dreams

In emerald dreams, life's tapestry weaves,
a symphony of hopes and whispering leaves.
Paths glimmer beneath the sun's warm gleam,
guiding us through each unfolding dream.

Through valleys deep and mountains high,
we laugh, we cry, we reach for the sky.
In emerald dreams, we chart our way,
guided by the light of each new day.

Within our hearts, a fire burns bright,
igniting passions, dreams taking flight.
With every step, each choice we make,
a dawn emerges in emerald wake.

We dance in hues of joy and green,
embracing all that life has been.
In this fleeting world, a precious seam,
revealing truth within each dream.

In emerald dreams, where time transcends,
a world of wonder that never ends.
Secrets whisper in the fragrant breeze,
unveiling mysteries among the trees.

We wander through enchanted lands afar,
where wishes bloom like the brightest star.
In emerald dreams, the past still gleams,
and futures shimmer with endless schemes.

Beneath the moon's soft silver beam,
we chase the shadows of a fanciful dream.
Through rivers of crystal and meadows green,
we wander freely in a surreal scene.

We strive for heights unknown, untold,
where emerald stories slowly unfold.
With courage as our steadfast guide,
we face our fears and set them aside.

In emerald dreams, we find our song,
a melody of belonging, sweet and strong.
Let us savor each fleeting gleam,
and hold tight to our emerald dreams.

# Leaving the Table

In a world where kindness once firmly stood,
now it wavers, teetering on fragile boards.
A table set with echoes of disdain,
where manners crumble like drops of rain.

Amidst the chaos, we build resilience,
strengthening our hearts, reclaiming brilliance.
For in the face of disrespect's bite,
we rise, reclaim our power, and ignite our light.

Once a place of grace and care,
where souls converged, hearts laid bare.
Now cloths are torn, words sharp as knives,
bitter fragments shadowed our lives.

In this new chapter, we stand tall,
mending cracks, bridging the fall.
With compassion guiding where honor presides,
we seek a table where dignity remains.

When respect is gone, and kindness swerved,
it's time to rise, claiming what we deserve.
To leave the table where bitterness stayed,
and find a place where joy won't fade.

For what is a table without respect?
A hollow seat, a bond unchecked.
No longer break bread with the unkind,
no longer linger, leaving light behind.

We search for another, warmth in hand,
where souls can sit and hearts understand.
Life is too brief for bitter bites,
for swallowing darkness, soaking in spite.

At the table we leave, our worth reclaimed,
nourishing our souls, never the same.
When honor fades, our spirits endure,
a place where kindness shines bright.

With courage as guide, resilience in stride,
we claim our space, no need to hide.
For when honor vanishes, our spirits endure,
we find the table where joy is deserved.

# Street Lights

Beneath the moonlight sky, they shine so bright,
those street lights guiding my wandering sight.
Whispering secrets upon the darkened road,
their glow encasing memories that once flowed.

Yet as you speak of these lights, dear friend,
a contradiction I struggle to comprehend:
How can they remind you of who I am,
when you never walked beside me, never took a stand?

The lonesome street lights continue to glow,
casting their luminous halo, an eternal show.
You stood apart, distant from the scene,
and now you claim I've changed — how unforeseen.

They illuminate paths where we once tread,
lost in conversations, dreams, and threads.
But you were absent; your presence gone,
so tell me, how can you judge me alone?

These street lights, faithful guardians of the night,
could have witnessed our friendship, basking in their light.
But you didn't witness, you were never near,
and now you accuse, fueled by unfounded fear.

The night sky weaved tales, as we danced on the street,
yet you say I'm no longer the friend you'd meet.
But darling, it was you who never took the chance,
to bask in the glow of this nocturnal dance.

Let the street lights keep on shining bright,
a silent witness to our journey, day or night.
I've remained the same, unwaveringly true,
but your absence, dear friend, affected the view.

# Moving Mountains

In the realm of uncertainty and strife,
two souls entwined in the dance of life,
one reaching high, the other low,
a tug-of-war of emotions, ebb and flow.

Amidst the shadows, a question lies:
is it truth or just a disguise?
Love's labyrinth, a complex maze,
yearning for change in countless ways.

Caught in a cycle of love and pain,
grasping for solace, all in vain,
until clarity shines its guiding light,
and in letting go, we find our might.

Standing at our best and at our worst,
the mornings after storms, when silence bursts,
longing for a fresh start, a brand new way,
can we rebuild what's gone astray?

Yearning for depth in each *'I love you'* said,
to plumb the heart, beyond the head,
moving mountains of emotion, bridging the gap,
yet feeling trapped in a stormy trap.

Once felt you cared, we once shared,
now wrestling with ghosts, feeling unprepared,
lost in a storm of emotions, deep within,
the echo of laughter now thin as wind.

Striving to shift the very earth beneath our feet,
clutching at hope amidst retreat,
as progress wanes and fades to gray,
finding ourselves adrift, in disarray.

In the quiet, in unspoken word,
reaching out, though voices unheard,
beneath the tumult and the strain,
a fragile chance to heal, to love again remains.

Seeking to break free from this slow descent,
fighting to hold on, against the torment,
mountains rise, jagged and impossible,
yet still we climb.

The higher the mountain, the thinner the air,
and all the weight of goodbye feels unfair.
Apologies falter, words fall short,
yet in the heart's battle, we hold our fort.

And in the end, one refrain remains:
*why leave me stranded in these mountainous plains?*

# Neon Dreams

In the heart of neon lights that never fade,
where dreams come to life under the arcade,
this city screams your name in vibrant hue,
a playground for the bold, the wild, the true.

Fortunes rise and fall in a single glance,
amidst the glitz, the glam, the fleeting chance,
where stars are born beneath the desert sky,
while hours slip past and nights fly by.

Music plays until the break of dawn,
a symphony of hopes and fears withdrawn.
Secrets linger in the glowing light,
a mesmerizing dance through endless night.

In every sidewalk restaurant and bustling street,
where strangers and friends inevitably meet,
this city is a tapestry woven with care,
each thread a memory, each knot a dare.

Through every neon glow and bustling street,
this city pulses — vivid, wild, complete.
For in its depths, I found peace with you,
in this city of dreams, bold, wild, and true.

# From Heartland to Heights

Paycheck to paycheck,
that's how we grew up.
From those Midwest cities,
where the wind carries stories,
and the sidewalks have worn grooves,
from the shuffle of dreams deferred.

They expected us to be screw-ups,
mismatched pieces in a puzzle,
left scattered on the floor.
Yet in the corners of our homes,
we stitched together hope from scraps,
a tapestry of resilience,
woven from the fabric of everyday life.

In the morning light,
families plotted the day's journey,
fingers tracing budgets,
eyes scanning the horizon for opportunity,
like hawks circling open fields,
searching for signs unseen,
waiting for the seasons to change.

In kitchens warmed by love,
meals were not just sustenance;
they were gatherings,
moments frozen in laughter,
the aroma of spices,
fading worries pinned on the wall,
like old photographs of places,
we never really visited.

On playgrounds of chipped paint,
we learned the rules of tetherball,
and the inexorable weight of disappointments —
every victory celebrated,
every loss a lesson whispered
by the leaves of the sturdy oaks
watching over our small ambitions.

They saw us as statistics,
but we felt the pulse of potential,
hearts beating to a rhythm
only we could hear,
echoing against the backdrop
of factory lines and endless fields,
where moonlit skies cradled our secrets,
and we forged dreams that soared
above rooftops, higher than coal dust clouds.

Growing pains etched our skin,
marks of tenacity and yearning;
we are not screw-ups, but survivors,
carrying the weight of history
and the spark of rebellion,
each dollar earned a step forward,
each setback a pause
before the next leap into the unknown.

In the swirling currents of time,
we rise, we fall, but we do not buckle,
no longer entangled in the nets
of narrow expectations,
we are the stories of flight,
spilling ink on pages of tomorrow,
writing new chapters
that take root in fertile ground,
where hope grows in abundance
amidst the rugged terrain of our upbringing.

Now here we stand,
grounded in the lessons learned,
facing forward, heart wide open
to the world of possibilities,
weaving our tales
from the fabric of struggles,
turning each paycheck into a promise,
refusing the narrative,
reclaiming our birthright
from those who saw us as lost.

In the embrace of dreams,
and the warmth of laughter,
we'll show them who we are,
not just from those Midwest cities,
but from every breath we take —
crafting futures from ashes,
transforming struggle into strength.

# Stories Woven in Time

In the mirror of time, reflections linger.
Looking back becomes a form of moving on.
Each lived moment opens its own passage,
history breathing beneath the present.

We do not carry the past as burden,
but as thread —
pulled through joy, through loss,
binding what was to what remains.

Some memories return softly:
hands once held, voices now absent,
love that taught us how to stay,
grief that taught us how to stand again.

Time continues—unmoved by sorrow,
seasons turning without permission.
Yet echoes persist, steady and familiar,
keeping us from unraveling completely.

The road ahead bends where it must.
Hindsight sharpens what hope once blurred.
Every crossing, every fracture survived
quietly instructs the next step.

We open the pages of yesterday
not to linger, but to honor—
each memory a testament to endurance,
proof that we have lived fully.

Life is not a straight line,
but a weaving:
joy knotted with grief,
resilience stitched through loss.

Still, the music carries on —
unresolved notes, imperfect harmony,
until love gathers what remains
into something whole.

What endures is this:
a life not spared from breaking,
but carefully reassembled—
a story woven in time, and kept.

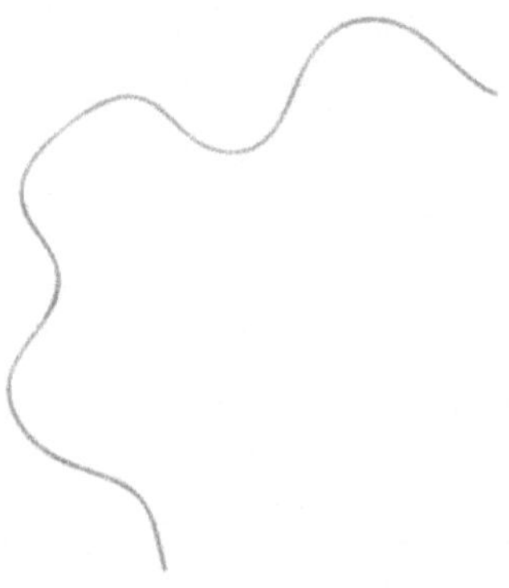

# DEATH

*The silence between breaths.*
*The ache of remembering.*
*The grace of letting go.*
*What ends, too, becomes part of the thread.*

# Everything was Gray

In a world of shadows cast in gray,
Where colors fade and dreams decay,
His hair — a silvery trace of age,
Smoke swirls softly in muted rage.

Lost in thought, his dreams turn cold,
Stories untold, quietly unfold.
My life entangled in his silent despair,
In a monochrome abyss, stripped bare.

A lie that binds us, twists and weaves,
Through hollow nights and haunted eves.
Everything I see is drained of hue,
A world without a vibrant view.

He wanders lost in a colorless maze,
Unaware of life's unyielding blaze.
Everything is gray, a muted scene,
A somber veil, a life unseen.

Yet, in the stillness of the gray,
Whispers of hope begin to sway,
Through cracks in the weary facade,
A glimmer of light, to never see day.

Echoes of the past flicker and gleam,
Shadows dance within a dream.
Even here, in this desolate space,
A fragile bond still holds its grace.

Though the canvas is painted bleak,
He once stood strong, his soul unique.
In the depths of this heavy haze,
A quiet mercy softens the gaze.

Everything was gray, yet light remains —
A fragile hope amidst the pain.

## Shades of Serenity

Following wise words I was taught to believe,
*"Money isn't everything,"* yet tempted to deceive.
I'll sell my soul for fortune, if it grants me liberty,
but in death's shadow, riches lose their dignity.

What remains, after striving tirelessly every day?
Amid life's reel, a radiant display.
Six-digit offers whisper with tempting sound,
yet triumph feels hollow when no peace is found.

Then came a call that altered fate's design,
three minutes enough to redraw the line.
Lost in the silence, despair took its place,
an unseen ache I could scarcely face.

Yet within the sorrow, a flicker held fast,
hope spoke softly — the night would not last.
In every trial, a lesson to find,
resilience awakening in heart and mind.

Embrace the journey, both valley and peak,
for growth often thrives in the moments most bleak.
The reel of existence plays scene after scene,
through courage and faith, life grows serene.

In the quiet whispers of the midnight air,
I reflect on the path paved with care.
Lessons learned from the choices made,
in the symphony of life, a melody played.

Through the storms of doubt and fear,
a strength emerged, quiet yet assured.
Grace revealed in the struggle's embrace,
a hidden beauty time cannot erase.

The clock ticks onward, relentless and true,
each moment a canvas, a shade, a hue.

Opportunities linger where shadows creep,
waiting to waken from dreams too deep.

In the dance of time, a rhythm unfolds,
in every trial, a story told.
The journey continues, winding and steep,
with each step forward, a promise to keep.

Soar high on dreams that dare to ignite,
let passion lift wings into endless flight.
With hope as your anchor, courage as guide,
let love be the thread where all truths reside.

And when the final curtain draws near,
may serenity banish every fear.
For in echoes of memory, soft and clear,
the beauty of life will reappear.

# Navigating Sorrow

In the depths of sorrow, my heart does weep,
grief consumes me, shadows vast and deep.
I stare at empty chairs, silent rooms,
haunted by echoes of absent tunes.

Brown round eyes, wide as Cyclops stare,
searching for a presence that is no longer there.
Memories flood, relentless as the tide,
faces and voices that death has pried.

The candle flickers, a solemn, wavering flame,
whispering softly, calling your name.
Each breath heavy, a weight I cannot lift,
death has stolen you, leaving me adrift.

I wander through the halls of our shared days,
each corner echoes your vanished ways.
Your laughter lingers in the air like mist,
a cruel reminder of all I have missed.

Grief wraps me in its relentless shroud,
a quiet scream, muffled and loud.
The night is endless, a void without end,
where life and death silently blend.

I speak to your spirit in the silent night,
a conversation with absence, veiled from sight.
The wind carries your laughter, faint and cold,
stories untold, hands I cannot hold.

The river of life flows, relentless, unbound,
yet in its current, your presence is found.
In shadows of twilight, I see your face,
a fleeting vision, gone without trace.

Through tears, I navigate this barren land,
grief as my compass, a trembling hand.
Death may claim bodies, but cannot erase,
the mark of a soul, its enduring grace.

In the silence of night, I feel you near,
a ghostly comfort, both tender and severe.
I trace your memory through the misted air,
and speak to the void, knowing you're there.

Death, the final chapter, yet not the end,
for love and memory refuse to bend.
Through sorrow's depth, I learn to grieve,
to honor, to remember, and quietly believe.

The heart broken, yet still it beats,
carrying echoes of departed feats.
Through shadowed valleys and midnight skies,
I navigate sorrow where my true love lies.

In each whispered wind and falling leaf,
I find traces of your soul, my relief.
Death may have taken your body away,
but your spirit walks with me, every day.

So I let the tears fall, unrestrained,
a river of mourning, love unfeigned.
And though your voice is silent, the room still cold,
in death's embrace, a story forever told.

# Shadows of Grief

Racing thoughts, a shock too deep,
a heartache overwhelming, impossible to keep.
They reminded you time and time again,
he was in front of the door, a loved one to tend.

But fate had other plans, cruel and unkind,
leaving you shattered, with a heavy heart entwined.
The echoes of his laughter, now just a distant memory,
leaving you with an ache that refuses to set free.

In the quiet moments when the world slows down,
the pain hits like a wave, making you drown.
You long for his presence, his comforting embrace,
but all that's left is an empty space.

Shock and heartache, a heavy burden to bear,
but in time, wounds heal and you'll learn to repair.
Hold onto the memories, cherish them dear,
for love transcends, even in moments of fear.

Through the darkness, a glimmer of hope will shine,
guiding you through the grief, one step at a time.
As the days pass and the healing begins,
remember love endures, through losses and wins.

In the whispers of the wind and in the morning light,
you'll find moments of peace, amidst the night.
Though sadness lingers, and tears may fall,
strength will rise, standing tall through it all.

Embrace the journey, the ups and the downs,
for in the depths of despair, strength is found.
And though the pain may never fully subside,
love's eternal flame will forever abide.

# Twilight's Whisper

In the shadow of twilight's embrace,
Mr. Dewitt's words now hauntingly trace.
A forewarning of life's fleeting grasp,
as moments slip through fingers fast.

"*There's a cold wind blowing,*" he did say,
and with each passing year, we stray
further from care-free jaunts of youth,
lost in time's relentless pursuit.

Should have listened, oh how we regret,
as aging's touch we cannot forget.
The best night of our lives, now in sight,
but slipping away like a fading light.

In the dance of shadows, death does call,
a reminder of life's transient sprawl.
For in the end, we all must part,
leaving behind a beating heart.

Cherish each moment, hold it dear,
for time is a thief, cold and severe.
Listen to wisdom's whispered breath,
embrace life's beauty before its death.

Engulfed in memories of days gone by,
yearning for that nostalgic sigh.
But time moves on, relentless and cruel,
leaving us adrift in its endless pool.

Each sunrise brings a chance anew,
to seize the day, embrace the view.
Let not the shadows of doubt descend,
choose joy and love to fiercely defend.

In the tapestry of life, woven and spun,
threads of hope and dreams are sewn.
Against the backdrop of fate's design,
our choices ripple through the grand design.

So fear not the passage of time's swift gait,
for within each moment, we create our fate.
Let laughter ring out, love resound,
in the symphony of life, profound.
Embrace the mystery, the unknown,
for in its depths, our souls are grown.
With courage as our guiding light,
we'll traverse the twilight, bold and bright.

# Echoes of Grief

In the silence of the night, grief whispers untold,
a void where your presence once shone bold.
No farewell spoken, just absence profound,
a silence more piercing than any sound.

Memories linger, whispers of what used to be,
now shadows in the dark, haunting endlessly.
Tears fall like rain, washing pain away,
yet the ache remains, a heavy price to pay.

Through sorrow's corridors, we seek our way,
finding solace in fragments of yesterday.
Grief is a journey, a river we wade,
where love and loss mingle in twilight's shade.

Though time may soften, the void remains,
the imprint of absence in lingering chains.
Yet in these echoes, a quiet hope gleams,
love threads the darkness with delicate seams.

Each passing day, a gentle reminder,
of the love shared, in hearts we find in each other.
Wiping away tears, with each sunrise we meet,
embracing the memories, our connection so sweet.

In every whisper of the wind, and in every gentle rain,
we find your spirit, soothing our deepest pain.
Though shadows cast long, over valleys so deep,
our love shines bright, a treasure we keep.

Through the darkest nights and the **brightest** days,
in our hearts, your presence forever **stays.**
The echoes of grief shall slowly **wane,**
replaced by joy, like sunshine after **rain.**

So let us hold on to the love we hold **dear,**
in the echo of memories, so crystal **clear.**
Together we'll walk, hand in hand,
embracing the future, where hope **forever stands.**

# Ghosts of Yesterday

The pictures have come down, the walls now bare,
memories of past days, now rare in the air.
The lingering ghost of smoke fills the room,
reminding me of days wrapped in a deep gloom.

Memories in plastic bins, a life packed away,
each step I retrace with a familiar sway,
your sad-eyed glance still haunts my mind,
a trace of you I cannot unwind.
The clock ticks slowly against the wall,
echoes of laughter, faint and small.
Shadows stretch where voices fell,
in this empty space, shadows cast and sprawl.

The chair still waits, but you're not there,
a silent witness to the vacant air.
Conversations gone, unfinished, unsaid,
whispers lingering where we once tread.

Timing and structure once clear as day,
now muddled, lost in fear's disarray,
losing and failing, flailing helplessly,
everyone's gone, missed marks barely seen.

In the midst of chaos, emotions expand,
the world so quick to judge, but too late to understand.
Struggling to make sense, losing grip on command,
navigating through this grief-stricken land.

I smile and pretend that I'm okay,
the charade won't last, it will fade away.
The walls still whisper of what's been lost,
love remembered, but at such a cost.

Now silence settles where laughter lay,
ghosts of yesterday will never stray.
Their shadows linger, etched in the night,
a memory's echo, just out of sight.

# Waltzing Flames of Love

In a dance of waltzing flames, we swayed,
embroidering memories time can't erase.
*"Twin flames,"* we whispered, hearts unafraid,
a passion fierce, untamed, ablaze.

With steps we knew so well,
we journeyed through time's embrace,
but sometimes truth can be hard to tell,
and reality paints over grace.

In a moment of starry-eyed delight,
we felt a glow like never before,
legendary love blazing bright,
from one kiss to forevermore.

Through twists and turns, we lost our way,
in a cemetery of lost dreams,
still alive, yet never quite at bay,
living in the echoes of silent screams.

You, the officer and gentleman,
me, the restless heart in need,
in a world of black and white, we stand,
bound by a love that's rare.

Whispers in the wind, telling me I saved you
but when the walls came crumbling down,
you knew how to take me to hell too.

Illusions fade and ink bleeds dry,
promises shattered, like broken glass,
a con man's deception, a lover's high,
leaving behind a love that couldn't last.

Courage roared in a final goodbye,
the lion's defiance, a silent cry.
Through braids of deceit, we sighed and died,
a love once blazing, now cold as stone.

In dreams engulfed in fiery mire,
we watched our field of poppies go up in flames,
a love that once burned bright with desire,
now reduced to ashes and remains.

What a valiant roar, what a tragic fall,
a love so fierce, yet unable to stand tall.
In the end, beneath truth's quiet sky,
even flames must learn to die.

# Tethered in Memory

Luck of the draw — yet always unlucky,
fate dealt its hand with fingers so clumsy.
If the story is over, why am I still here,
writing new pages in absence and fear?

The writing on the wall bends in the wind,
tracing the spaces where our story thinned.
Your voice a shadow, your laughter a ghost,
a love now a memory I cherish the most.

Through months of tears, we fought our own battles,
each step forward carried a weight of sorrow.
Windows reflecting the questions of why,
a chair left empty, your cup untouched,
moments suspended, memories clutched.

If life is a story, its pages now torn,
I scribble the blanks where your memory's worn.
Threads of you woven in every fragile line,
a tethered delight, even in decline.

The moonlight spills cold on empty chairs,
and I speak to the air as if you were there.
Yet only silence answers, steady and deep,
a sorrow that lingers, refusing to sleep.

Time moves in circles, relentless and slow,
yet grief anchors me where I cannot go.
Every echo of you pulls at my chest,
a ghostly embrace I cannot rest.

Through grief and through loss, I stagger and bend,
finding in memory both wound and friend.
For though the world moves and days drift away,
your absence resides in the night and the gray.

In the quiet dark, your lessons ignite,
guiding me forward, through endless night.
Though the chapters close and years move on,
your shadow lingers, never fully gone.

# The Gift of Sadness

In the depths of despair, a flicker of light,
a whisper that pain can still birth right.
Death has lost its meaning if we do not know
how to truly live, and let our blessings show.

There's purpose in pain, though it hides from sight,
a quiet resolve in the heart's long fight.
You seek a reason for what you've endured,
but what if your pain is the purpose assured?

For sadness is a gift — no shield from ache,
but a lantern of truth in the path we take.
So walk through the storm, with all its tests,
for in each struggle, the soul manifests.

Let your wounds tell stories of grace, not defeat,
a triumph found where sorrow and courage meet.
Through shadows of doubt, we find our way,
emerging stronger with each passing day.

Embrace the healing power that comes from within,
turn anguish into wisdom, let your soul begin.
Like a phoenix rising from ashes anew,
transform your pain into strength, let it imbue.

In every tear, a lesson quietly taught,
in every heartbreak, a battle bravely fought.
For in the darkest hour, we find our spark,
emerging from the depths, luminous in the dark.

# Melodies of Solitude

In the darkness of the night, I reach for the phone
Dialing your number, hoping you might be home.
I've called more times than I'd care to admit,
Just to hear your voice, a balm for my spirit.

I listen to the gentle cadence of your speech,
On your voicemail, your name is a melody within reach.
Melancholy seeps in as memories flood my mind,
Tears fall like rain, leaving heartache behind.

In the echoes of your voice, I hear a hidden pain,
A soft whisper of sorrow amidst the refrain.
I analyze each intonation, each sigh that escapes,
Capturing the essence of longing, as my heart reshapes.

Though distance divides, your voice stays near,
A solace in silence, a comfort through fear.
I keep calling, listening, holding each word,
Clinging to echoes I've already heard.

Goodbye was unsaid, but the silence spoke it clear,
Tears that fell like raindrops, washing away my fear.
I'm left with memories, clinging tightly, holding dear,
Each precious moment a treasure to endear.

As the days turn to weeks, and weeks into years,
I'll whisper your name, through laughter and tears.
Our bond unbroken, by time or space,
A connection cherished, in life's hectic race.

I'm going to miss you, forever it seems,
Lost in the echoes of broken dreams.
But in my heart, your presence will stay,
Guiding me through each passing day.

# Light in Sorrow's Shadows

In the midst of sorrow's heavy weight,
I found a glimmer of light today.
A laughter bubbled up, pure and bright,
for the first time since you went away.

The world kept spinning, moving on,
offering condolences for a time.
But as days blur and weeks drift past,
support fades, and life resumes its chime.

Yet within the silence of loss and grief,
I discovered a new way to breathe.
Learning to carry the memories with grace,
as I navigate this ever-changing maze.

So I laughed today, with all my heart,
finding joy in a world torn apart.
For in the midst of sorrow and pain,
I will keep going, even through the rain.

In the echoes of yesterday's bittersweet hue,
I seek solace in moments that felt true.
Glimmers of hope in a sky painted blue,
amidst the clouds of gray that often brew.

Each tear that falls, a whispered release,
each smile that dances, a fragment of peace.
In heartache's embrace, strength takes increase,
a quiet resilience, a subtle masterpiece.

As time marches forward, never standing still,
I carry your memory, a beacon until
the rays of healing climb the distant hill,
and the wounds of grief begin to still.

So in laughter and tears, I find my way,
charting a course through the darkest day.
For in the midst of sorrow and pain's bitter reign,
I'll keep pressing forward, without refrain.

# A Legacy of Love

One day, the news will come,
and hearts will pause mid-breath.
Phones will ring,
faces will pale,
and the quiet weight of absence
will press into the rooms we occupy.

You will live in voicemails,
replayed with a trembling care,
in photographs on shelves
that catch dust and sunlight alike,
and in the hollow of chairs
where laughter once lingered.

The void will stretch wide,
but it will be stitched
with memory —
the smell of your favorite coffee,
the way your keys jangled in the morning,
the echo of a laugh
that could lift the heaviest hours.

You were a presence, irreplaceable,
a pulse threaded through ordinary days,
a hand that steadied,
a glance that understood.
Even in absence, you are here.

Your light remains in the music we play,
in the streets you loved to wander,
in the books you cherished,
and in the quiet pauses
when the world feels too heavy
and we remember who you were.

And though grief will visit
with its heavy cloak,
we will also celebrate —
the laughter you inspired,
the courage you taught,
the warmth that never fades.

Your legacy is love
woven into the fabric of our days,
a light that guides
when the world grows dim,
a presence that whispers
through every memory,
every shared glance,
every heartbeat that remembers.

You belong here,
your place secure,
forever in our hearts,
always pure.

# The Art of Being

In shadows cast by thoughts of final fate,
I find a mirror, urging me to appreciate.
Death's stark gaze invites quiet introspection,
a call to savor life and every connection.

Each heartbeat echoes a precious refrain,
a melody of joy that rises through the pain.
For in mortality's cold, embracing hold,
we learn to cherish every grace untold.

Let us not let the days slip away,
but seize them in the golden light of day,
to live with purpose, love with open heart,
and carve from life's vast tapestry our art.

Embracing the beauty of each moment passing,
in life's symphony, our spirits ever amassing.
A dance of shadows and light intertwined,
eternal echoes of the heart and mind.

Let gratitude bloom within our souls,
nurturing kindness, where compassion rolls,
like a river of love flowing endlessly,
binding us together, setting us free.

Cherish laughter, embrace the tears we share,
and know that in love, we are always there,
connected by threads of fate and destiny,
woven tight in humanity's tapestry.

# Tangled Rhythms

In a dance of addiction, we find ourselves caught,
you crave the fix, but I'm the one that's sought.
Toxicity lingers in the air we breathe,
a battle that no one truly leaves.

You chase the high, while I chase your healing,
filled with love, yet my pain keeps revealing.
Your cup overflows, mine remains bare,
trying to change you, but drowning in despair.

You consume me till I'm gasping for air,
giving my all, with nothing left to spare.
Your pleasure, my pain, the cost of connection,
lost in a cycle of our endless affection.

You need me, yet crave the bottle more,
I offer my help, but I'm left feeling small,
while you stumble, I break your fall.
Hopeless in my devotion, yet always in vain,
caught in a cycle that brings only pain.

The rush you seek, the side effects I bear,
in this twisted dance, it's a heavy burden to bear.
Yet still I stay, unable to break free,
bound by love, memory, and history.

In the depths of desire, we both drown,
held captive by each other and spiraling down.
Trapped in a tango of give and take,
the fragile thread of our bond starts to break.

Your laughter echoes joys long past,
my heart aches, paying the emotional cost.
Seeking solace in the shadows we cast,
love tainted by a future fading fast.

Lost in the maze of our tangled emotions,
we navigate this labyrinth of unspoken devotions.
A dance of contrasts, light and shade,
a fragile balance on which we've laid.

Your addiction, a symphony of highs and lows,
while my heart bleeds with silent woes.
In this twisted dance we call our own,
we struggle to find a way to be shown.

Falling deeper into the abyss we create,
struggling to break free, to escape fate.
Yet in the chaos, in the storm we form,
we still find warmth — love's quiet, fleeting form.

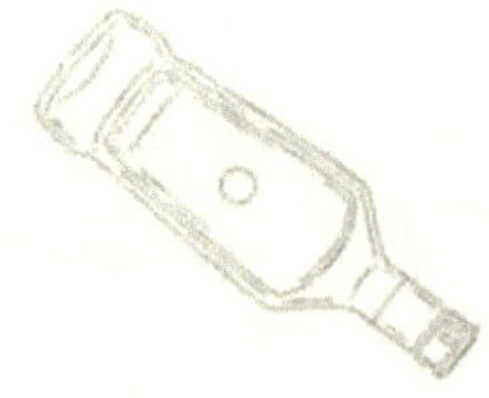

# Shadows of Solace

In the shadows, loneliness dwells deep,
a currency of absence, too costly to keep.
Silence whispers truths, painful and stark,
a reminder of absence, a void in the dark.

I mourn the life you didn't get to live,
the dreams unfulfilled, the love to give.
Memories of you, a bittersweet embrace,
more years without you, time and space.

Like currency no longer in circulation,
I navigate the ebb, the quiet isolation.
Loneliness and grief entwined in my heart,
aching for you, worlds apart.

Echoes of laughter, now faint and thin,
sorrow and longing weave quietly within.
Pieces of you scattered across the past,
across the memories that forever last.

Desolate paths I walk, searching for a sign,
invisible threads connecting your heart to mine.
Yearning for a touch, a voice, a gleam,
lost in the realms of an unending dream.

The weight of absence, heavy and unkind,
a cycle of loss etched deep in my mind.
Yet amidst the shadows that cling to my core,
I find moments of solace, memories to restore.

# The Gift of Time

Time is not a thief.
It does not steal what's ours to keep.
It gathers quietly — moments, memories,
traces of love too sacred to repeat.

Think not of what it's taken,
but of what it's given —
the warmth of mornings once shared,
the sound of laughter still hidden in air.

What if time is the source,
and grief the true culprit.
A shadow cast upon a generous light,
confusing loss for what still lives inside?

Time gives us all it can muster:
the rise, the fall, the breath between.
It does not fade or flee;
it overflows — unseen, serene.

It is not sinking away,
but spilling over,
so full we cannot hold it all,
and mistake its abundance for departure.

Time is only good,
that's why we ache to find it again,
to trace its rhythm, to feel its grace,
to catch what was never meant to end.

Because time was never lost.
It lingers in the hush of memory,
in the pulse of what was loved,
in the echo of every name still whispered tenderly.

# The Weight of Empathy

In a world of fleeting joy and pain,
my heart beats to a quieter strain.
I feel the cries of distant others,
their suffering echoes like rolling thunder.

I cannot turn from their silent pleas,
their struggles crash like relentless seas.
Empathy grows, a weight I bear,
their unseen burdens, their whispered prayer.

Each passing day, it presses near,
the sorrow between, so sharp, so clear.
I hold their hurt, their pain I share,
their silent struggles, their unspoken care.

Yet in this empathy, I find a gift,
a connection that inspires and uplifts.
For in feeling their pain, their despair,
I offer solace, to show I care.

Let me carry this burden of grace,
a reminder of life's ties, embrace.
The pain we share, the hearts we mend,
a quiet bond that will never end.

# Cherished Echoes

He was out of his pain,
I was drowning in mine.
Lost in sorrow, seeking solace, I could not find.

Through the darkness of our separate storms,
two souls adrift, longing for guidance.
Whispers of longing, fragile as smoke, our hearts still spoke.

His burden weighed heavy, dragging him down,
while I struggled to keep from sinking, to not drown.

In his absence, memories cascade like rain,
echoes of laughter, overshadowed by the pain.
I light a candle, a beacon in the night, guiding his spirit, a comforting
light.

Through time's vast expanse we endure,
bound by threads of fate, seeking a cure.
Our paths intertwined, a dance of destiny, navigating the labyrinth of
uncertainty.

In life's tapestry, our colors blend,
moments of joy mingling with sorrow's end.
Yet hope flickers like a steadfast flame, guiding us through hardship,
calling our name.

In the symphony of existence, our melody plays,
notes of resilience amidst the disarray.
With each verse sung, our tale unfolds, intertwined journeys, stories
untold.

We march onward, facing the unknown,
finding strength in the depths we have grown.
Embracing the light, letting courage shine through,
together in spirit, steadfast and true.

# Whispers of Loss

In the depths of sorrow, a heartache resides,
his life cut short, leaving me shattered inside.
Memories tucked away in storage bins,
pretending it's okay as the loneliness begins.

He was sinking, I was rising high,
I burned the linens, tears staining the sky.
Cried in public places, solitude overgrown,
feeling so casually cruel, facing it all alone.

Days drift by as the clock ticked slow,
echoes of his laughter continue to grow.
In the still of night, his absence profound,
I wish he were here, happy and sound.

Shadows dance in flickering light,
whispers of his voice haunt me at night.
I grasp at memories, fleeting like wind,
searching for solace, a new beginning to begin.

Through tears and pain, I seek a trace
of light in darkness, a familiar face.
In the depths of grief, I cling to hope,
believing that one day, I'll find a way to cope.

# Tears & Transcendence

As I touched down on unknown ground,
sunglasses shield my eyes from dark skies,
tears fall silently as I walk through CLE,
each step a new pierced hole in my heart.

Lost within the city's maze of concrete and steel,
I seek solace in the echoes of the past,
memories whisper through the wind,
guiding me through this unfamiliar path.

In the shadow of towering buildings,
a glimmer of hope breaks through.
Light seeps into the cracks of sorrow,
illuminating a path toward healing.

The doors of the funeral home opened as I approached,
more paperwork to sign,
there it was, multiple times,
cause of death in black and white.

Yet amidst the grief, the sun still rises,
casting a golden hue on my tear-stained face,
whispers of love linger in the air,
a reminder of the joy that was once there.

Through the quiet streets, I wander,
lost in a sea of unfamiliar faces,
yet a sense of belonging creeps in,
reminding me that I am not alone.

Amidst the chaos, a moment of calm,
a bench in a quiet park beckons me near,
the statue of Mother Mary looks on,
underneath the shade of ancient trees,
I find solace in nature's symphony.

In the distance, the church bell tolls,
a bittersweet cadence marking time.
Each chime a tribute to those departed,
each echo a memory that refuses to fade.

As I sit down to rest in this familiar yet new place,
I feel a glimmer of peace wash over me,
a gentle reminder that in letting go,
I find the strength to carry on.

# Threads of Fate

Beneath a sullen moon, my heart whispered low,
a shadowed echo in the night's quiet glow.
When I endured loss, a whisper amidst the din,
I asked myself, could there ever be meaning within?

Through sorrow's veil, my eyes began to see,
the fragility of life, its uncertainty.
A truth emerged, whispered soft and cold,
of limits we face, of stories age-old.

In the labyrinth of existence, where paths intertwine,
I discovered, in essence, a pattern, not divine.
Yet threads fray at the edges, seams may tear,
revealing how fleeting hope and care can be.

Within this contrast, I found a tender truth,
between control we seek and the fate of youth.
What truly matters slips like stardust in the night,
Yet for a moment, I held it with all my might.

As I ventured deeper into my soul's vast domain,
I uncovered parts, touched by an indelible stain.
Scars etched so deeply, time could not conceal,
whispering tales of pain only the heart could feel.

I stood beneath a streetlight flickering awake,
rain threading through my sleeves,
rereading the last message you sent
until the screen went dark —
that small silence teaching me
how endings really arrive.

In my journey through the night's embrace,
I found grace in fragility, and beauty in the space.
Though parts of my soul bear scars, raw and real,
through cracks in our armor, the heart still learns to heal.

# Tears in Twilight

In this dim-lit corner, I quietly seek,
praying everyone in this bar doesn't see
the two black lines running down my cheek,
blurred trails where joy used to be.

Glasses clink, and laughter sails,
yet my mind is lost in darker tales.
In shadows, grief and I become well-versed,
a somber, twisted, heart-wrenching dance.

The world outside moves fast and bright,
but I am anchored in this endless night.
Voices blend, yet none discern
the quiet message my silence yearns.

Memories, like ghosts, around me swirl;
in their grip, I am a helpless, embattled girl.
Every moment marked by what's amiss,
a heavy weight, a silent abyss.

Through the haze, a flicker of light—
a distant hope, fragile but clear,
a reminder that pain, no matter how severe,
finds its match in the courage to persevere.

The melody of my heart, now a minor key,
harmonizing with the sorrow of what will never be.
Yet, within this cocoon of despair,
I find a strange, comforting solace there.

Amidst the grief, the sadness, the strife,
lies the quiet, undeniable strength of life.
A whisper soft, echoing low,
reminding me that even in suffering, we grow.

As I sit beneath twilight's glow,
allowing myself to feel, to truly know:
even as tears freely flow,
the darkest night eventually lets the light show.

# I Knew Before it Happened

In the quiet of the night, whispers echo in my mind,
"*Yes, I already know the answer,*" a truth I cannot bind.
But I'm not yet ready to accept it, to let it take its hold,
for the reality it brings is a tale too cold to unfold.

Everything I was afraid of happening, happened in the end,
fears realized, dreams shattered, with no way to mend.
Back to the days when I would make believe you were still near,
wishing for a moment, a sign, a whisper in my ear.

Memories like ghosts haunt the corners of my soul,
a bittersweet reminder of a love once whole.
Yet the answer remains the same, a truth I cannot deny,
I must face the pain, the loss, and bid farewell to the lie.

So I stand here alone, with a heart heavy and worn,
knowing the truth, though it leaves me torn.
Yes, I already know the answer, clear and bittersweet,
but in my heart, your presence I'll always meet.

In the stillness of the night, a symphony of whispers weaves its way,
echoing truths I hold dear, yet reluctant to believe.
The answer lingers in the shadows, a secret untold,
a truth so profound, too heavy to hold.

With each passing moment, the inevitable draws near,
a tapestry of emotions, threads of hope unclear.
I grasp onto hope, a flicker in the dark,
yearning for a chance, a new, hopeful spark.

Faced with the echoes of past sorrows, I find solace in the pain,
for in loss, there lies wisdom, a lesson gained.
As memories dance like shadows in the night,
I embrace the truth, a beacon of light.

Here I stand amidst the echoes of our past,
embracing the solitude, the die now cast.
In the depths of my soul, your presence will forever reside,
a comforting solace, a love that cannot hide.

# Celestial Connections

It's the realization
that I may spend more years of my life
remembering you
than I actually had with you.

I stared at the sky tonight,
the moonlight over the city lights meant so much,
to know there's one thing in life
that one will never touch.

Memories flood my mind
with bittersweet embrace,
what was once present,
now lingers as a trace.

Time slips like sand through hands,
leaving echoes of a distant land.
Days turn to nights,
seasons come and go,
yet longing for you
continues to grow.

In the depths of my soul,
your presence remains,
a melody of love,
an unending refrain.

Beneath the skyline,
teardrops glint in my eyes,
whispering to the night
where my heart still lies.

Though you are gone,
your essence lives on
in the tapestry of my life,
where you belong.

Stars shimmer,
their light a gentle reminder of your grace,
a celestial thread
time cannot erase.

I lose myself in the vast expanse,
searching for your spirit
in every cosmic dance.
The moon's gentle glow
guides me through memories,
helping me cope.

As the world moves forward,
I cling to the time shared,
the words left unsaid.
Through whispers in the wind
and dreams in the night,
I hold your presence
in my heart's quiet light.

In life's journey, with grace and song,
I weave your legacy
where you belong.

# Solitary Adieu

In the shadows of my mind, a whisper softly grew,
somehow I knew, deep within, I'd never again see you.
Yearning for a life once had, a question lingered through,
a part of me wondering if what once existed was true.

Through tear-stained eyes, I see the truth so stark and blue,
why must parting come, so final, so true?
Farewell drifts on the wind, a solitary adieu,
leaving me to navigate this life without you.

A void, an absence, louder than any spoken word,
echoing in my heart, a silent, sorrowful chord.
Goodbye was unsaid, yet the silence speaks it clear,
I'm left with memories, clinging tightly, holding dear.

As time moves on, and life's pathways shift and skew,
I'll treasure what was once had
though you are gone, in my heart, you'll forever renew,
a part of me still lingers, longing for you.

Memories replay like echoes through the night,
every laughter, every smile, a quiet, glowing light.
In life's vast tapestry, our thread once new,
now weaves a past both beautiful and true.

Seasons change, offering subtle, gentle cues,
embracing the cycles, bidding a fond adieu.
I'll carry on, the memories ensue,
a tribute to the life we once knew.

# 8:29

At 8:29, the news shattered calm —
A three-minute call, a world disarmed.
Shock and questions clouded the air,
Balance lost in despair's tight snare.

I fell to the floor, grief gripping tight,
Tears cascading through the morning light.
How could this be? Why such a twist?
Answers vanished in a deep emotional mist.

Through shock and grief's heavy veil,
In a daze of loss, my heart grew frail.
The mind in disarray,
Grasping for answers, lost in dismay.

The weight of loss, so raw and deep,
Leaving a void the shadows keep.
Memories entangled — joy and sorrow,
A life rewritten in a single breath.

In grief's harsh grip, we cling to light,
Through wrenching sobs, through endless nights.
Seeking refuge in a storm so wild,
Holding on to the memory of a smile.

Rest in peace, yet remain near,
Your presence felt, though no longer here.
Life unraveled in a blink of an eye;
At 8:29 a.m., the heart learns to cry.

Stillness comes in the quiet storm,
Guiding us through this broken form.
And in the echoes of sorrow and pain,
Love endures, like a gentle refrain.

# Moonlit Melancholy

Beneath the midnight moon's soft glow,
you clung to the bottle, lost in woe.
But I won't wake beside you tomorrow,
our bond now steeped in regret and sorrow.

You say I left without a care,
yet all along, I longed for love we could share.
The karmic cycle ends with the curse's sting,
as fate tore us apart, unraveling its ring.

The queen in your deck, once poised and bold,
now broken, a symbol of stories long told.
Our paths diverge as the night grows colder,
a chapter closed as we both grow older.

Through whispers of wind, our laughter fades,
shadows consume the love we made.
A tapestry stitched with unwept tears,
guiding us through our silent fears.

The stars bear witness, silent, pale,
to the wreck of a love, a bittersweet tale.
Though the tide has claimed what could not last,
may peace find us, release the past.

As pages turn and night moves on,
our story retreats, its colors withdrawn.
Farewell to what was — we face the unknown,
in the hush of the moon, we walk alone.

# Two Graves

All roads led me here,
to this hollow moment of love and fear.

When they asked how I was doing,
I didn't know what to say —
my silence betraying a heart in decay.

The night unwinds what daylight spun,
a tapestry unmade,
thread by thread undone.

Our story frays, the fabric thin,
a love that once held
now caves within.

You said you couldn't live without me,
and part of me hoped that was true.
Yet if you saw me now,
you'd think I moved on —
but every time I was with him,
I imagined it was you.

The damsel is depressed,
the knight long gone.
Two graves
in this tragedy we built upon.

When you fall apart,
you never quite fall back together the same.
I wore a crown —
a queen with a broken frame,
trying to be strong
while the world grew so hard.

I gave so many signs,
love's silent plea,
yet you couldn't turn things around —

a decree
I couldn't fight,
couldn't defend.

Now silence
is all that remains
in the end.

It was real enough to get me through,
but even real things wither too.
You had my six,
once steady and true,
but even shields crack
when loss cuts through.

The story is over,
yet I keep writing pages,
echoes lingering
through endless ages.

The road less worn calls my name tonight,
its quiet edges soft
beneath my hesitant feet.
I trace the path
I was too afraid to take,
wondering how far
it would have carried me.

And the beautiful little fool I was,
still searching for meaning
in what never was.

Our love —
its vows, its fire, its unrest —
now laid to rest.

Yet even in death,
I carry the sound
of a love once whole,
now underground.

# Unfinished Chapters

In your arms, I fell apart so easily,
yet you should have held me closer, breathing gently.
Our foundation, fragile, made of broken promises,
it's time to face the truth, no longer to dismiss.

We navigated chaos, caught in endless conflict,
but I am slipping away, my heart conflicted.
I offered grace in your troubled land,
yet you still managed to let me down, I could not withstand.

As days bled into nights, we tried to mend
the fractures of a bond that would not bend.
Whispers of doubt grew louder in the silence,
a once-treasured connection now meeting defiance.

Each tear shed became a river of regret,
a weight upon my chest I could never forget.
The pain and sorrow etched upon my face,
a love once cherished now lost in the maze.

At the edge of goodbye, I stand alone,
echoes of what was, a solemn tone.
In the end, the pain outweighs the grace given,
leaving behind a heart, bruised and unforgiven.

A story left unfinished, a chapter closed,
yet memories linger as the darkness imposed.
Through grief and despair, a new flame ignites,
in the ashes of love, hope claims the nights.

So farewell to what once was, a bittersweet end,
a journey of love we could not defend.
Yet in the depths of loss, life quietly survives,
for every goodbye births a chance to rise.

# If Heaven is Real

If heaven is real,
I hope you don't miss me
as much as I ache to see you here.
I hope the air is gentle with you,
free of regrets, free of sadness,
and that the silence stretches soft and peaceful
like a calm sea under golden light.

I hope when you arrived,
a wave of forgetfulness swept over you,
washing away the weight of pain,
leaving you entirely full of life,
laughing in the corners of clouds,
dancing in sunlight unbroken.

I hope you yearn for nothing,
no one to tether you to the past,
no shadows, no ache —
only the warmth of eternity's embrace.

Perhaps I feel both of our grief as one,
a weight pressing upon my chest,
and if that is so,
it only means you are here with me,
and I am strangely okay with that.

I hope grief has no residence there,
no echoing chambers of longing,
only quiet joy that hums
beneath the endless sky.

And maybe, sometimes,
I wander into your dreams,
a whisper, a familiar hand,
reminding you that here,
we are not truly apart.

I hope in heaven you found
the peace I always wished for you,
the kind that settles deep in the bones,
that makes laughter easy,
that makes sorrow impossible.

And if heaven allows,
perhaps one day
I'll see the light in your eyes again,
and we'll meet in that quiet space,
where love lingers
and time cannot take us away.

# Midnight Cabernet

In the darkness of night, when the world is still,
a whisper of grief lingers, a heavy chill.
Midnight Cabernet, poured in a glass,
a balm for the soul, a moment to pass.

Each sip a memory, bittersweet and true,
a tribute to lost ones, whose time flew.
The weight of their absence, an ache profound,
in the quiet of night, their whispers resound.

Grief keeps me company in borrowed light,
a quiet weight I carry through the night.
Tears gather gently, unnamed, unsaid,
old battles echoing what the heart has bled.

Past and present blur inside this glass,
scars catching glimmers of moments past.
At the bar, I sit with doubts I can't outrun,
lost between what was and what's to come.

From dusk to dawn, their laughter returns,
a distant warmth the memory burns.
Love once held, now drifting apart,
locked in the chambers of a breaking heart.

Midnight Cabernet, a toast to the past,
to those we have loved, whose love will last.
As we navigate through sorrow's steep descent,
finding solace in the darkness, a moment well spent.

# Embracing Grief

In the garden of her heart, untamed and wild,
she sat with anger, like a wayward child.
Long enough to feel the tears, the pain, the strife,
and in that moment, she discovered her real life.

She learned her real name was grief, so deep and true,
a companion in the shadows, a friend she never knew.
With every hurt and broken piece she thought to keep,
grief whispered softly, in the silence, so deep.

But in the depths of sorrow, a seed was sown,
a tender shoot of healing, in the darkness grown.
For grief, her loyal companion, taught her to see,
the light in the shadows, the way to be free.

She rose from the ashes, a phoenix in flight,
embracing her grief, her sorrow, the fight.
And in that acceptance, she found her true self,
strong and resilient, like a forgotten book on a dusty shelf.

Tears fell freely, emotions flowed,
for grief is a teacher, a guide we all know.
And through the pain, the sorrow, the strife,
she learned her real name was grief, the essence of life.

# RESILIENCE

*From the ashes and the echo —*
*The will to rise again.*
*To mend, to remake,*
*to live, still.*

# A Beacon in the Dark

In the depths of despair, you came,
a steady hand, a gentle flame.
Through my faults, through all my fears,
you found the light through endless tears.

Through the storms, the nights so long,
you whispered hope, you made me strong.
Amid my doubts, my hidden pain,
you showed me sunshine after rain.

Your eyes could see what I could not,
the truth, the strength I'd long forgot.
When shadows fell and hearts grew cold,
your light remained, steadfast and bold.

Through every trial, every bend,
you were my guide, my truest friend.
Your kindness bloomed where hope seemed lost,
a beacon shining, no matter the cost.

I rise now with your light in me,
strong and steady, wild and free.
The path ahead may twist and sway,
but with your flame, I'll find my way.

Grateful for the stars above,
for sending me your steadfast love.
In the depths of despair, I see,
you were the one who believed in me.

# Dancing with Uncertainty

In the tapestry of life we weave our way,
through paths of light and shadows of gray,
uncertainty dances in the air we breathe,
leaving us lost, yet longing to believe.

When I'm yours, a fleeting moment spent,
but only for the long weekend, life's gift lent,
a taste of joy, a glimpse of what could be,
yet time drifts on, leaving hearts at sea.

We grasp at dreams, hoping they come true,
but life's twists and turns reveal a different view,
in the midst of chaos, we find our way,
seeking solace in the light of a new day.

Embrace the unknown, the ebb and flow,
for in uncertainty, our true selves grow.
Though the road ahead may be unclear,
let love and hope be your guiding sphere.

In the vast expanse of the universe,
we are mere travelers, a part of the great traverse,
each moment offering a chance for growth,
as we navigate the highs and lows of both.

The stars above twinkle with cosmic light,
guiding us through the darkness of the night,
reminding us of the beauty that surrounds,
even when life's uncertainties confound.

Let your heart be a compass true,
leading you to skies of azure blue,
where dreams take flight on wings of hope,
and courage helps us conquer life's tightrope.

Life's journey, a blend of contradictions,
some choices bring joy, others lessons.
Yet through it all, we learn and we thrive,
in the dance of uncertainty, we truly come alive.

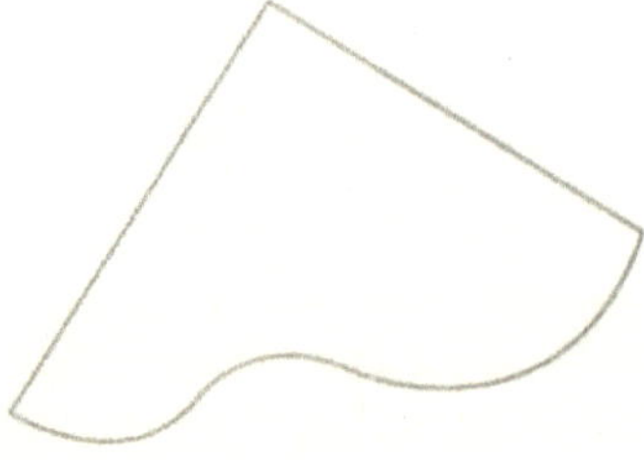

# Tempest of Heartache

One quiet day, when shadows grew,
the truth of us came breaking through.
There lies a story, deep within the rain,
of how you became the main source of my pain.

Once you were the sun, in my endless sky,
the warmth in my winter, the truth in my lie,
but as seasons changed, the glow turned thin,
and night swept in where day had been.

You, once my compass, guiding me through,
transformed to a storm, cold and untrue.
The laughter we shared, the dreams we'd proclaim,
faded to whispers, shadows of blame.

In the garden of trust, where our love took root,
the blossoms of care bore the bitterest fruit.
Every word, every touch, that once felt so right,
turned bitter with silence, in the endless night.

The mirror of love, once polished and clear,
cracked under the weight of what could have been.
I gazed into the fractures, seeking a sign,
only to find your shadow, no longer mine.

The stars that once guided us fell out of line,
distant, indifferent, refusing to shine.
You became the storm, relentless and wild,
leaving me adrift, in the tempest, exiled.

Yet from the wreckage, a truth takes form:
even the weakest can weather the storm.
For within the darkness, a spark will remain,
a seed of resilience born of the pain.

Now I rise from the rain, scarred but aware,
forging new strength from the weight I bear.
For though you became the ache I must wear,
within me blooms the power to repair.

# Praying Tonight

She's waiting praying he doesn't die tonight,
clutching the phone, knuckles white,
pacing the rooms, steps worn thin,
a storm of fear, a war within.

Thoughts spin of what she did and didn't say,
moments lost, words gone astray.
A heart heavy, time stretching long,
each second hums a fragile song.

Every second lingers, stretched and long,
the sterile air hums a mechanical song.
From somewhere afar, a monitor beeps,
its rhythm steady, a fragile heartbeat.

The hallway echoes with hurried strides,
doctors and nurses pass, hope collides.
Shadows stretch beneath fluorescent glow,
fear grips tighter, refusing to let go.

Whispers of hope echo through her mind,
a fragile thread she clings to, intertwined.
Undying faith in miracles, she longs to find,
though doubt presses hard, she will not unwind.

She bargains with heaven in a trembling plea,
*"You can have it all — just let him be."*

Through darkness and despair, she finds her way,
resilience forged in the fire of day.
With every breath, strength is renewed,
a beacon of hope in solitude.

For within her beats a heart of unyielding power,
fueling her spirit, hour after hour.
This journey may test her, push her to her core,
but she knows deep down, she can endure more.

With every breath, she gathers strength anew,
resilience, her armor, guiding her through.
For even in the darkest night, she'll find a way,
to hold onto hope and embrace a brand new day.

As she waits, praying he doesn't die tonight,
her resilience shines bright, a beacon of light.

# Defiant Spirit

In the face of judgment, she stands tall and free.
To hell with opinions, they hold no decree.
She moves to her own rhythm, fearless, precise,
painting her world with courage, no need to be nice.

Her strength is unyielding, her spirit unbound.
She walks through the darkness, refusing the ground.
The whispers of doubt, the voices of disdain,
dissolve into silence, she outgrows the pain.

With every sunrise, she wears resilience,
a practiced disguise, quiet defiance.
Beneath every mask lives a truth she defends,
unbroken. Unwavering. This is who she is.

To hell with your opinions, she says without fear.
Her worth isn't measured by who's watching or near.
Her circle is small, but it's loyal and rare,
a sanctuary built from love and repair.

Judge her not for the battles you missed,
for the nights she survived, for the scars that persist.
She is a warrior of light in relentless dark,
grace in her step, fire in her spark.

In life's living tapestry, she stitches her name,
threaded with courage, not shame.
Each obstacle met with deliberate grace,
a testament written in how she stays standing.

Through storms of adversity, she holds her ground.
Unbowed. Unbroken. Unmoved by the sound.
The echoes of doubt, the shadows that loom,
she meets them head-on and empties the room.

With every step, she leaves evidence behind,
a mark of power, deliberate, defined.

Her presence a force, her voice a vow,
a courage that echoes — then and now.

To those who doubt, to those who scorn,
she offers no proof, she's already reborn.
In the crucible of living, she forges her truth,
a warrior of light, unfiltered, uncaged.

Let the critics chatter. Let the cynics sneer.
She knows her worth — undeniably clear.
She stands in her truth, unwavering, bright.
To hell with your opinions — she is the light.

# Eye of the Beholder

Look in the mirror.
You've gone out of your mind,
because you're out of mine.
Distorted reflections,
fragments of laughter and tears,
swirling in the glass,
fingers tracing the outline,
of a face you barely recognize.

What does it mean to lose oneself,
to drift in liminal spaces,
where thoughts wander like aimless ghosts,
fading in and out of clarity?

A tapestry unraveled,
threads of memory slashed,
each day a new knot to untie.

Once, you strolled the streets
with purpose behind your eyes,
an anchor in the storm,
finding warmth in the sun.

Yet now,
echoes of voices chase you,
whispering doubts like shadows,
leaching color from your spirit.

You search for reason,
in the silence that blooms like wildflowers,
between the heartbeat of the day and night,
but all that answers
is the hollow ring of solitude,
an empty room in your mind,
where dreams go to flicker and die.

Look deeper.
Eyes are windows,
reflecting not just visions,
but the tapestries woven from whispers,
each crease, each line,
a story, a battle, a song,
you may have forgotten the melody,
yet the rhythm still thrums beneath.

In the quiet thunder of tumult,
a sparrow sings for you,
a reminder that freedom
can be captured in fleeting moments;
the way dew rests on grass blades,
delicate, unburdened by time,
yet shimmering with the weight of all it holds.

Breathe in the stillness,
let it cradle your spirit,
for the mind is a labyrinth,
twisting paths of thought and emotion,
but there is beauty in every corner,
a glimpse of clarity
amid the chaos.

Stand before that mirror,
gaze into the wildness of your soul,
you may feel shattered,
but pieces can heal,
forming a mosaic —
a portrait vibrant and alive.

Look again,
beyond the fleeting shadows,
colors still await your hand.

A canvas opened wide,
the world arms extended,
waiting to show you
that the journey within
Is where truth ignites,
kindling the spirit,
and guiding you home.

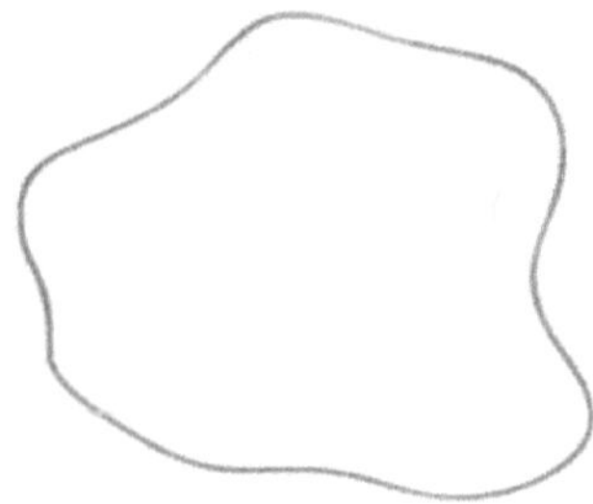

# They Call Me Strong

People love to call me strong,
as if it's a badge I asked to wear,
as if resilience were a crown I chose,
but the truth is, I didn't choose this path —
it chose me.

I walked it because there was no other way through,
through storms that cracked open parts of me
I didn't know existed,
through pain I had no time to process,
through falls from heights I never imagined.

And yet, from the rubble, I rose,
stronger than I thought possible,
but never by choice, never by ease.
I never wanted to be tested like this;
I never wanted to learn strength through survival.

My strength didn't come from never breaking.
It came from breaking —
shattering into fragments,
then rebuilding,
time and time again.

It comes from standing steady for others
when my own ground gave way beneath me,
from smiling through storms
while my heart was a hurricane.
When you call me strong,
know this:
I became this way
because falling apart
was never an option.

And even now, when the world weighs heavy,
when doubt creeps in like shadows at dusk,
I carry forward — not because I'm unbreakable,
but because I have been broken,
and I have chosen to rise.

Strength, I've learned, is not a gift — it's forged.
In fire, in loss, in the quiet of sleepless nights.
It is not polished or perfect,
it is raw, it is jagged,
it is the echo of every time I refused to surrender.

So yes, call me strong.
But remember the cracks, the scars, the nights I survived.
Call me strong,
but know that my power
was born in the breaking,
and in the courage to keep walking through it all.

# Inner Warrior

In the quiet of the night, under the stars so bright,
how amazing is it, a solo battle we fight,
not against enemies or foes out there,
but against the doubts and fears we bear.

To be at war with nobody but yourself,
seeking inner peace, pursuing inner wealth,
confronting our shadows, embracing the light,
navigating the darkness, seeking what's right.

In this journey of self-discovery and growth,
we face our demons, uncovering the troth,
learning to love the flaws we see,
embracing our truth, setting ourselves free.

May we be warriors in our own right,
challenging ourselves, reaching for new heights,
how amazing is it, this inner quest,
to be at peace with oneself, feeling truly blessed.

With every step we take along this road,
through valleys deep and mountains we've climbed,
we find the strength within ourselves to hold,
and the courage to leave our doubts behind.

Amidst the chaos and the noise of the world,
we seek solace within our souls unfurled,
embracing the silence that speaks so loud,
guiding us through this internal shroud.

With each battle won, we grow stronger still,
embracing the journey, embracing our will,
discovering depths we never knew,
becoming the heroes of our own story, true.

Let the stars above continue to shine bright,
as we walk this path through the dark night,
for in the silence, in the depths of our soul,
we find the strength to make ourselves whole.

# Rising Strong

In the quiet of morning,
the sun spills gentle light,
like soft whispers cutting through fog.

I sit with heavy thoughts;
they swirl around me,
a storm I never wished to invite.

I remind myself:
do not let the shadows
claim the seat at the table.

The heart is vast,
and I am learning —
learning to clear the clutter,
to breathe through the chaos,
to seek out the corners of joy
hidden beneath the weight.

In healing my mind,
I've healed my heart.
With every anxious breath,
a thread weaves
a tapestry of resilience,
each moment stitched with courage.

Through wavering melodies of doubt,
I find the rhythm of strength.

The heart beats strong,
a warrior in its own right,
against whispers that say:
*I am weak,*
*I am alone,*
*I am unworthy of the light.*

But I am stronger than I think,
a flower pushing through concrete,
each petal unfurling against the chill,
rooted deep in resolve,
drinking from the well of hope.

And when anxiety comes,
a familiar visitor —
I turn and face it,
no longer a prisoner
to its heavy cloak,
but a sculptor of my own peace,
chipping away at the stone of fear,
shaping it into strength,
into armor that glimmers in the dawn.

I am the architect of my thoughts,
the gardener of my spirit,
tending the soil,
pulling the weeds of negativity,
letting light in,
whispering to myself:
you are enough,
you are whole,
you are loved.

Anxiety, once a storm,
is now a river that carries me,
its current a reminder that I am alive,
flowing forward,
transformed by the very thing
that once threatened to drown me.

Each day a new canvas,
brush in hand,
I paint with every choice,
with every breath:
colors of hope,
shades of strength.

I remind myself:
*I am the artist here,*
*the one who chooses light in shadows,*
*the one who sees beauty in scars.*

And so I walk
through fields of my thoughts,
the wind at my back,
carrying whispers of strength.

With each step,
I reclaim the ground beneath me,
I reclaim my joy,
a journey unending,
as I rise —

a sunrise in my own heart,
brighter than I ever believed possible.

# Fierce Resolve

She didn't need guidance or advice,
the lessons were hers to learn,
and nothing anyone offered could spare her the fire.
She felt the pain
and wore it deliberately,
like the stilettos she wore everyday.

In sorrow's silent grasp, she stood firm,
unfazed by well-meaning words that crashed like waves,
there was no script to follow, no map to trust,
only her own hand on the wheel,
her heart set steady on the horizon.

The lessons came slowly,
etched through trial and heat,
unearthed only by walking straight through.
Pain kept pace beside her,
a quiet companion she never denied.
She dressed it in confidence,
let it echo in each deliberate step,
every stride a testament to her strength
as fate spun wildly around her.

Through loss and triumph, she moved forward,
grace tempered by grit,
light unextinguished.
This path was one she drew herself,
her story written by her own hand,
day after relentless day.

She welcomed the unknown with fierce resolve,
turning hardship into ground where growth took root.
From chaos, she evolved.
From setbacks, she rose.

She basked in the warmth of her own flame,
a beacon of resilience in the dark.

With every setback, she'd rise and reclaim,
her power radiating like a spark.

And so she danced through life's winding maze,
with courage as her shield and love as her guide.
Every twist and turn, she'd boldly face,
with unwavering strength by her side.

While the world offered its condolences, she knew it was moot.
She didn't need guidance or advice;
the lessons were hers to learn,
and nothing anyone could do would change that.

The lessons were carved deep,
unearthed only through trial and fire.
There was no map, no rehearsed script,
only her heart as compass, steady, unyielding.

She welcomed the unknown with fierce resolve,
turning hardship into ground where growth took root.
From chaos, she evolved.
From setbacks, she rose.

She burned with her own flame —
not loud, but lasting.
And still, she danced through life's winding maze,
courage at her back, love as her guide,
meeting every turn head-on,
unwavering.

# Resilience, Here You Are

**Originally read at a 9/11 memorial commemoration in Jersey City, NJ (2022).*

Life moves us,
challenges day by day,
not allowing us
to know our fate.

Awakened each day
to more possibilities,
new voices laced
with interesting stories.

Hammered by stress and trials,
we cannot live in denial.
Learning and growing are essential.

When there are cracks in the foundation,
we stare life in the face.
Defeat we may taste,
but we stand in the storm,
not fearing harm, and in the end,
we will continue standing tall.

When we are not sure where to focus,
and it seems most prudent
to be rigid and fixed in place,
yet unyielding and closed is really more about saving face.

Remember, inside of being rigid and fixed,
also lives the agility of flexibility,
with the ability to learn and grow,
for what's in store, you may not know.

So remain open to what's at your door,
a metaphor, yes, of a life well-lived,
and loving of all that's coming,
a becoming of something more.

For you are a light in the darkness,
in a world that's full of both regardless.

So choose wisely on the path,
and stand tall in the aftermath,
where pain may act like a chain of a dance that's past,
and release yourself from that notion,
as it is an unlikely potion,
because on the other side of pain is motion,
and a joy so splendid it need not be mended,
only tended and defended,
just like the light.
As you know, through the resilience,
you are the knight on a dark night.

And may we always keep in mind,
throughout our daily grind,
the spirit of those we lost,
who paid the ultimate cost.

# Unfiltered Truths

In a world of laughter and cheer, where joy abounds,
some seek tales of hope, of dreams unbound.
But I yearn for the darker truths both raw and bold,
the stories of struggle that shaped who we are.

Tell me not just of the fires that shaped your soul,
but of the tempests that took their toll.
Of storms endured, battles fiercely fought,
for in those moments, your strength is sought.

I crave the unfiltered truths of your past,
the scars that healed but forever last.
Share the depths of your heart's strife,
the wounds that carved the edge of life.

Take me on the journey of your life's terrain,
through valleys of sorrow and peaks of gain.
Let me walk beside you and learn,
from the twists and turns where courage burns.

In your trials and pain lies wisdom untold,
lessons lived, stories of courage bold.
Don't hide your heart — let your story flow,
from hardship, resilience begins to grow.

Recount the moments lost and won,
when despair outweighed the sun.
It's in the shadows that strength is found,
where courage rises from the ground.

Share your fears, your grief, your pain,
the moments when hope seemed to wane.
Through struggle, might is revealed,
and wounds once raw are slowly healed.

Let your story unfold, a tapestry grand,
woven with courage, stitched by hand.
In your journey, I see reflection,
a search for truth, a deep connection.

As we navigate life's turbulent sea,
we embrace the challenges that set us free.
For in the darkness, we find our greatest light,
guiding us forward, shaping our sight.

# Choosing Connection

In the realm of time, we sway and bend,
dying once, but living every day.
Through fleeting moments, we weave our way,
building bridges or walls with each step we lay.

I know we don't know one another anymore,
but that doesn't mean I don't hope you get home safe,
even if I don't know where home is for you these days.
I hope you still find peace, the quiet moments, and look up at the sky,
the blue and gray haze.

Choices before us, like whispers in the wind,
do we seek connection or just pretend,
that barriers and boundaries shall be our end, or will we choose unity,
our paths to blend?

I hope you landed the life you wanted,
even if it's so different than the one I chose.
Life is a canvas, vast and true; do we build walls or bridges to renew?

Each day a chance, a boat set afloat,
toward a future where love keeps us aligned.
In the currents of time, both fierce and mild, we navigate the journey,
tender and wild.

Seeking connection, more precious than gold,
our shared stories are waiting to unfold.
Let our hearts awaken, our spirits rise, choosing compassion,
open and wise.

Let bridges endure, unshaken, unbent, anchored in care,
built with intent.
May we choose wisely, in each step we take,
for our own hearts' sake and those we embrace.

Let our actions be kind, love a quiet flame, guiding each day,
lighting a world to reclaim.

# Reflections of Transformation

In the mirror I see a different face,
not the one I once embraced.
A transformation deep and wide,
within myself, I chose to reside.

You do not know me as before,
I am reborn, I have much in store.
Embracing change that's overdue,
reintroducing the new me that's true.

Nobody gives power, it's just there,
take hold of it, show you care.
Failure leads to paths unknown,
out of comfort, we have grown.

If they don't value your presence near,
grace them with absence, dear.
My circle small, but true and bright,
friends who answer, day or night.

I moved on, not in spite or hate,
but to love myself, set straight.
Caring for me, holding the key,
to a life that's authentically free.

With each new dawn, potential glows,
now I walk where confidence flows.
Challenges met with head held high,
fulfilling dreams that touch the sky.

A journey of self-discovery embarked,
embracing flaws, no longer stark.
Strength found in vulnerability,
shining with inner authenticity.

Let the winds of change blow strong,
in transformation, we all belong.
For in the mirror, we often see,
the person we're becoming, free.

In the midst of change, I find my way,
navigating through each passing day.
With a heart that carries a heavy bane,
for it's not like I forgot about them, I'm just dealing with the pain.

In the mirror, I gaze deep,
reflections of the past, promises to keep.
A soul evolving, shedding old skin,
embracing the journey I begin to win.

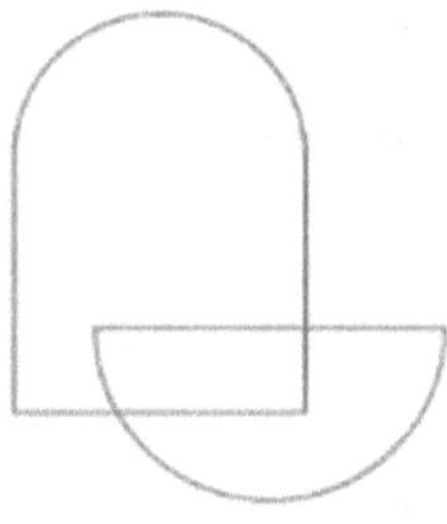

# Hidden Gardens

In the hidden gardens of the soul,
where shadows play and silence bleeds,
lies a path less traveled, rugged and steep.
Here, the quest is one of courage, a story untold,
learning to love and heal — the bravest role.

With every step, a whisper in the wind, soft and slight,
carries tales of battles fought long into the night.
Amidst the struggle, a truth too often missed:
healing emotional scars is a journey that persists.

No guidebook gifted, no map to mend the heart,
only pieces of a puzzle, each a jagged part.
The process, winding, sometimes unkind,
demands patience, grace, and an open mind.

Time, they say, can heal the deepest cuts,
yet loneliness haunts the hollows and ruts.
The ache of memories, tender and raw,
the longing for closure — etched into every flaw.

Yet in this odyssey, there's beauty in the pain,
in every tear shed, a chance to love again.
For in the fabric of our being, woven tight and true,
lies strength to recover, to rise from what we knew.

Wanderer, take heart, let this truth be known:
you are not alone on this road you own.
Though it takes a lifetime, fret not the hours,
for what was broken can bloom into flowers.

When weariness strikes, lost in the night,
remember, after darkness comes the first fragile light.
Embrace the journey, let it shape who you are,
for in loving and healing, we bear our brightest scar.

# Embrace, Heal, Transform

In the depths of your heart, feelings reside,
never can you run from what's deep inside.
No vacation from wounds that tear you apart,
face your angels and demons, make a fresh start.

Embrace your vulnerabilities, imperfections in tow,
your heart, a treasure you must get to know.
Work on emotional health, tend to your soul,
heal your wounds, make brokenness whole.

In the grand scheme of life, suffering is not the key,
no need to list every trauma for all to see.
Turn your pain into kindness, a transformative art,
become a healing soul, that's where you'll truly depart.

In the labyrinth of emotions, they dance and collide,
in the ebb and flow of life's unpredictable tide.
Stirrings of joy and sorrow in a delicate balance,
embrace the whispers of your own beating heart.

Navigate through the shadows, find the light,
let courage and hope guide you through the night.
Embrace the unknown, let your spirit soar,
transform the darkness into light even more.

Every scar tells a story, a lesson to be told,
a testament to resilience, a journey bold.
Embrace the scars, they make you who you are,
a mosaic of experiences, a guiding star.

Let love be your compass, forgiveness your shield,
in the garden of compassion, let wounds be healed.
A symphony of emotions, a soulful song,
in the tapestry of life, where you belong.

Dive deep within, explore the depths of your being,
in the canvas of existence, begin freeing.
Plant seeds of kindness, nurture your growing heart,
in the vast universe of love, play your part.

# Closure

In the whispering winds of time, it's over.
A chapter closed, a tale complete, seeking closure.
Yet the heart yearns, it craves for more, no closure,
Wishing fervently, that it wasn't over.

Through the echoes of the past, it's over.
Memories dance, bittersweet, seeking final closure.
But a lingering doubt, a longing remains, no closure,
If only we could rewind, pretend it wasn't over.

The clock ticks on, relentless and sober.
Fate's decree, a final verdict, it's over.
Yet in dreams we find solace, a loophole, needing closure,
Whispers of what could have been linger, no closure.
In the silent shadows of the night, it's over.

Amidst the colors of dawn's light, it's over.
A new day dawns, with hopes anew and closure.
Yet amidst the brightness, a yearning stirs, no closure,
A desire for what once was, for it wasn't over.

In the symphony of life's highs and lows, it's over.
Notes of closure strike, their final bow, the closure.
But in the melody's sweet refrain, no closure,
Longing for a different tune, for it wasn't over.

In the tapestry of time we weave, it's over.
Threads of past and present entwine, the closure,
Though questions remain, the heart learns to grow —
Even without closure, we still move forward, it's over.

# Stars and Tears

In a river of tears, I find myself swept,
deep underwater, feeling so inept.
Will you watch me drown, or lend a hand?
On my knees, will you understand?

You once needed me, or so I believed,
but the bottle held a stronger reprieve.
Toxic codependency poisoned our space,
only revealed as I sought a new place.

You left me confused, unsure, and torn,
half a sentence, my heart worn.
Yet in your gaze, the truth quietly lay,
a sad tale unfolding in subtle ways.

I never confessed the nights I knew,
each slip, each sip that pulled you through.
Your restless quest kept me awake,
counting stars for the peace I'd take.

Surprising to see our paths diverge,
you sinking low, while I began to surge.
Dancing in my mind, in a room of gloom,
instead of the woods, where flowers bloom.

Our reflections in the mirror, so estranged,
forever changed, our lives rearranged.
In the shadows of our shared past, I find,
a tapestry of emotions woven in time.

Whispers of forgiveness carried by the wind,
soft echoes of what once had been.
Shattered illusions, scattered dreams,
reclaiming my soul, bursting at the seams.

In the silence of night, under starlit skies,
I gaze at the constellations, tears in my eyes.
Seeking solace in the vast unknown,
embracing the pain, letting it be shown.

Through the wreckage of a broken bond,
I emerge stronger, my spirit beyond.
No longer tethered to the weight of the past,
embracing the future, free at last.

# Dancing in Transformation's Light

In a world that shifts and sways each day,
your strength shines bright when you embrace the sway.
Greet new beginnings with an open heart,
release the old, and let courage play its part.

Change sparks growth, like flowers in bloom,
petals unfurling, dispelling the gloom.
Adapt, evolve, and lift your gaze high,
spread your wings and let your spirit fly.

Hold your head steady, let fear drift away,
face each challenge, let courage lead the way.
Within your heart, a quiet flame will glow,
illuminating the path where your true self shows.

Life's tapestry weaves past with today,
threads of experience guide each step of the way.
Ride the tide of change, embrace its chance,
each moment a rhythm, each breath a dance.

Sunrises carry whispers of renewal,
a blank canvas waits for your vision to fuel.
Embrace the unknown, let your spirit sing,
transformation's journey — a wondrous thing.

Ride the waves with boldness, unafraid of height,
let winds lift you toward brilliance and light.
In life's grand dance, find your guiding star,
a melody of strength, revealing who you are.

Let your soul soar, embrace the unknown,
within each shift lies the power you've grown.
Step into brilliance your journey ignites,
dancing freely in transformation's light.

# Shadows Where Memories Lie

In the silence of night, I remember us,
through sleepless nights, the tortured poet I became,
ink bleeding my pain, carving out my name,
parts I never dared to explore on my own,
yet you embraced them without control.

I can still smell the essence of your being,
memories lingering like a sweet embrace,
one of us remains in this place unseen,
while the other's heart wanders in a different space.

I asked you a question that lingers within,
*"How can one love without truly knowing?"*
But your silence whispered a truth untold,
leaving my heart in constant yearning and growing.

Who else decodes you, reads between the lines?
Invisible strings tie us, through space and time.
The things that haunt me in the middle of the night,
still shape the shadows where we reside.

Through months of tears, we fought our own battles,
each step forward carried a weight of sorrow,
but in hindsight, it's a mix of pain and laughter,
a bittersweet symphony of today and tomorrow.

Under the moonlight's gentle glow,
we dance amidst the shadows of regret,
realizing that some things we'll never know,
unreachable dreams we must learn to forget.

No weapon formed can break our spirit's might,
even amidst the echoes of past pain,
ghosts from your past, the monsters caught up to you,
yet wasn't it beautiful when we believed in everything we knew?

Wiping away tears, I find strength anew,
in the echoes of our shared past,
you were my home, my shelter, my call,
even without a physical hug that would last.

Though one of us remains, the other has flown,
to new horizons, leaving a lingering ache,
the story of us looks a lot like a tragedy now,
a flight risk with a fear of falling, I still don't know how.

Yet in the shadows where our memories lie,
I feel the pull to rise, to try.
Through sleepless nights and whispers of pain,
I find the strength to breathe, to remain.

# Triumph in the Inferno

In the dance of life's relentless blaze,
we tread through fire, lost in a haze,
courage our compass, we face each day,
confronting our shadows, come what may.

Through darkness deep, we chase the light,
seeking redemption in the endless night,
like Dante's soul in the Inferno's fire,
we rise again, climbing higher and higher.

Flames of chaos, secrets we bear,
yet in the end, strength finds us there.
Victory blooms where courage has tread,
a path reclaimed from the fear we shed.

With hearts held high, we walk anew,
embracing trials that test what we knew,
each stumble, each tear, each twisted turn,
shapes the soul, teaches what we learn.

Through valleys shadowed and peaks aglow,
we navigate life's ebb and flow,
in the weave of fate, in the threads of time,
our spirits ascend, resilience in rhyme.

We cherish the ache, the laughter, the strain,
for joy and sorrow are threads of the same chain,
every wound endured, every battle we fight,
forged in fire, we emerge into light.

So march on, steadfast, brave, and true,
the crucible burns, yet strengthens you,
from inferno's depths to the sky's vast dome,
we rise unbroken, and claim our home.

# An Ode to the Unspinning Life

What's the word for when your life stops spinning,
while the world spins on, indifferent, winning?
A whirlwind of time, life's ceaseless chase,
and suddenly a stillness takes its place.

Around you, motion carries on,
yet your own axis feels withdrawn.
*"What's the word for this?"* you whisper in despair,
when your life pauses, and no one seems to care.

A riddle unsolved, a feeling untold,
stark and unique, yet quietly cold.
Is it envy, festering deep in your soul,
as others sail forward while you drift out of control?

But envy poisons, a thief of delight,
and jealousy binds you, shrouding the light.
No, the word must be finer, sharper, true,
a name for the power that lies within you.

It's resilience, dear, strength from within,
rising through trials, letting new life begin.
When time pauses, and your world stands still,
you gather your courage, bending your will.

Life's not a race to match others' pace,
but a journey unique, a singular space.
Embrace this pause, this transient reprieve,
reflect, recharge, and learn to believe.

Though the world spins on, and chaos is near,
you move to your rhythm, guided by your own sphere.
Find solace in stillness, let it be your guide,
for life is yours to shape, with fire inside.

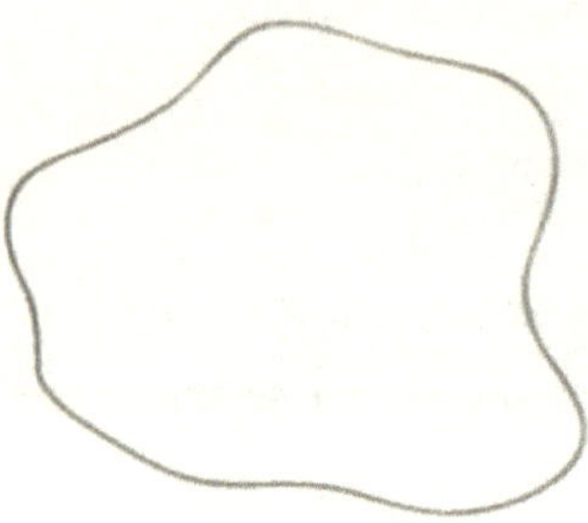

# A Raven's Cry

*Originally published in Poetry Downtown (2024), honoring Edgar Allan Poe.*

In the stillness of the night, the raven's cry resounds,
let its haunting echo serve as a solemn reminder, profound.
A cycle of life, where death and grieving pass like fleeting storms,
yet beauty emerges 'neath a stormy sky.

Through every sorrow, a glimmer of hope shines bright,
guiding us through the darkest of nights.
Let the raven's cry whisper tales of resilience and woe,
embracing life's cycle wherever we may go.

As we mourn what once was, let us also rejoice in what will be,
for death is not an end, but part of life's eternal decree.
Let the echoes of the raven's cry linger in the air,
a symbol of life's ever-turning wheel, beyond compare.

In the moonlit shadows, memories intertwine,
each whisper of the past a sacred sign.
The raven's cry pierces through the veil of time,
a reminder that even in darkness, light will shine.

With each passing moment, the world evolves,
lessons learned, problems solved.
In the symphony of life, the raven's call remains,
a melody of existence, amidst joys and pains.

May we listen closely to the raven's mournful song,
for in its sorrowful notes, we find where we belong.
The cycle continues, ever turning with grace,
as we navigate life's challenges, in every place.

# The Uninvited Guest

Pain, she enters, uninvited guest,
Brutal force, in turmoil dressed.
Without a knock, she storms the gate,
Leaves hearts in shambles, such is her trait.

A tornado fierce, through peace she tears,
With no regard for the rubble she bears.
No greetings fall from her icy lips,
No invitations to share sips.

In the heart's core, she takes her seat,
Devouring joy, making hope deplete.
Her feast — our feelings, tender and pure,
On our despair, she seems to endure.

We, her prey, caught in her snare,
Victimized by a presence so bare.
Solitude's cloak, around us she wraps,
In her darkness, our essence she traps.

Her power vast, a sight unseen,
Making significant souls feel unseen.
Alone, irrelevant, shadows we become,
Under her reign, relentlessly numb.

Yet, in her wake, a strength is born,
From our battles, a resilience worn.
Pain, though brutal, a teacher severe,
In her shadows, we learn to persevere.

For in our fight, our spirits ignite,
Finding in darkness, an ember of light.
She may visit, but cannot stay,
For we are always more than her prey.

In our hearts, a flame still burns,
With each strike, more brightly it turns.
We are more than victims of fate,
Within us lies the power to create.

Let pain come, let her do her part,
But never let her consume the heart.
For within us lies, a force untold,
Turning pain's stories into courage bold.

# Beneath the Masks

In a world full of masks and hidden scars,
I search for those with the most honest eyes,
drawn to the damage that lies beneath,
to the souls brave enough to let their truths rise.

There's a beauty in undressing, in exposing it all,
in embracing flaws and the pain endured,
for it takes courage to navigate life's falls,
and reveal the strength that lies obscured.

I crave the ones who grab life by its horns,
yet understand the power of vulnerability and pause,
those who've weathered relentless storms,
yet stand tall, whole, and unchained.

Give me those with hidden depths,
with pain simmering beneath the surface,
building up to be released in trust,
to someone who sees beyond the facade's purpose.

Show me your true character in the raw,
those with masked facades, let your true colors shine,
for in the authenticity of your being,
true beauty and strength you will find.

Let the scars speak of battles fought,
the trials faced and lessons learned,
for in the wounds of the past we find,
the stories of resilience and bridges burned.

In a world that often shies away from truth,
I seek the ones unafraid to face their past,
to acknowledge the pain and seek growth,
in the hardships that life so often casts.

Show me your depths and hidden fears,
let me see the struggles you've had to bear,
for it is in the vulnerability we share,
that true connection and healing appear.

Embrace the shadows that linger within,
for they hold the keys to our innermost self,
reveal the layers hiding your essence,
and in doing so, find liberation and wealth.

Let your guard down, be unafraid,
to show the world the beauty in your pain,
for it is in the rawness of our human plight,
that we truly connect and forever gain.

# Grit & Grace

In the face of darkness, they stood strong and tall,
braving the depths, they refused to fall.
Those who've returned from the brink, unafraid,
souls raw and exposed, yet undeterred they stayed.

Pressure, like that which forms a diamond bright,
no longer bound by falsehoods, no longer hidden from sight.
Lost dreams and shattered hopes, untethered from them now,
no longer bound by past, no longer held in doubt.

In moments of uncertainty, the mind does stray,
questioning the norms, doubting the readily accepted way.
The outcasts and black sheep, running from the world's cruel glare,
their words unspoken, their pain too much to bear.

There's something to be said, but words can't heal all wounds,
scars remain unhealed, despite time's gentle turns.
The spirit pushes past its breaking point, striving to find its light,
for there can be no pearl without first enduring the grit's might.

To those who've faced the dark and survived,
their strength and resilience, a testament to the undying drive.
For in the midst of chaos, they found a way to shine,
a beacon of hope, showing they rise through every trial.

# The Shattered Mirror

In him, I found a mirror so clear,
reflecting all that I hold dear.
The real, the raw, the highs, the lows —
a light within my heart that glows.

Unafraid of faults displayed,
I longed to join his quiet serenade.
Hand in hand, through shifting sand,
we dreamed a life we'd understand.

For in his world, I found my place,
a sanctuary of love and grace.
Together, we'd weather any storm,
our bond unbreakable, steadfast and warm.

Everything I saw, all that I've known,
in him, a love distinctly grown.
With him, I'm whole, complete, unfurled,
captivated by his world.

Then cracks appeared, unseen at first,
missteps and words, our bond reversed.
The mirror shattered, splintered pain,
our harmony now echoes strain.

The mirror shattered, reflecting pain,
the highs and lows now laced with strain.
Our quiet serenade turned into a discordant song,
our once steady bond now feels wrong.

Hand in hand, we stumbled and fell,
each misstep tolling like a bell.
Shifting sands became a maze,
we wandered lost in twilight haze.

Our sanctuary of love and grace,
now echoes with emptiness in its place.

Once unbreakable, now fragile and torn,
our hearts battered, weary and worn.

All that I held so dear and true,
slipping away, as emotions grew askew.
In his world, I once found solace and peace,
now a battlefield where conflicts increase.

Yet deep within, a flicker remains,
a glimmer of hope through lingering strains.
Captivated by what once was true,
yearning to mend, to start anew.

In chaos, in fragments, hope survives,
a quiet ember where love still strives.
Though the mirror is cracked, love remains,
softly enduring through sorrow's stains.

# Remnants of Us

In the darkness of the night, we burned so bright.
Our love blazed fierce, but faded out of sight.
We might have loved too much, lost in our own clutch.

Now it's over, no closure in sight,
left wondering in the still of the night.
Fighting in only your army, on the front lines,
defending all, ignoring the signs.

I'm a mess, tangled in our desires,
the mess you wanted, lighting our fires.
But now we stand, worlds apart,
with memories etched in every part.

Though we burned out, there's still a spark,
a reminder of when we danced in the dark.
For all that we were, and all that we lack,
I'll hold on to the moments, never looking back.

The echoes of our love linger on,
in the whispers of the wind before dawn.
The embers of passion slowly fade,
leaving behind a bittersweet cascade.

We once painted the night with our dreams,
now lost in the shadows, torn at the seams.
A love too intense, too wild to sustain,
leaves us both longing, filled with pain.

But in these ruins, I find a glimmer,
a chance to heal, to grow, to simmer.
Our story may have reached its final chapter,
but the memories will forever capture.

I'll walk this path, uncertain and new,
carrying remnants of me and you.
In the depths of my soul, you'll always remain,
a reminder of love, of loss, of gain.

# For She is Kintsugi

In the depths of darkness, she found her light,
a warrior adorned in gold so bright.
Through shattered pieces, she emerged whole,
for she is Kintsugi, with a resilient soul.

Each crack a story of trials endured,
yet she chose to rise, her spirit assured.
Fragments bonded with shimmering grace,
a masterpiece born from a broken embrace.

In life's crucible, she was tested and tried,
but from the ashes, true strength applied,
With every fracture, a lesson refined,
for she is gold, with resilience aligned.

Let her story be a beacon of hope,
a testament to the power to cope.
For she is Kintsugi, bold and unbowed,
a survivor's triumph, radiant and proud.

In the still of night, her spirit ascends,
guided by galaxies where infinity bends.
In the tapestry of time, she weaves her role,
a constellation shining, an eternal soul.

Each star holds secrets yet untold,
stories of courage, of love, and of old.
Connecting the heavens with deft finesse,
a stellar dance, a cosmic caress.

Through vast expanses, she boldly roams,
unraveling mysteries that lie in unknown domes.
With stardust in her veins, fate intertwined,
she is the universe, luminous and refined.

In the symphony of orbits, she finds her tune,
harmonizing with sun, moon, and monsoon.
Singing melodies of resilience and grace,
a cosmic aria that fills endless space.

Let her radiance blaze in galaxies afar,
a luminary of hope, a guiding star.
For she is a constellation of courage and gold,
a celestial ballad, beautifully bold.

# Light Amidst Shadows

In the heart's battlefield, where shadows loom,
the worst battles I've felt were between what I knew and what I wanted.
A tug-of-war between reason and desire,
where dreams and truths collide
and the edges of certainty fray.

Whispers of uncertainty cloud the mind,
as doubts and fears intertwine.
But amidst the chaos, a glimmer of light,
guiding the way through the darkest of nights.

Within the depths of passion's flame,
lies the essence of our hidden aims.
A constant dance of will and fate,
shaping our destinies, weaving our tapestry's state.

Through storms of doubt and winds of change,
we navigate this journey strange.
Finding strength in moments of weakness,
harnessing wisdom from times bleakness.

At the crossroads of choice and consequence,
we carve our path with every ounce of reverence.
For in the clash of knowledge and longing,
lies the chance for growth and understanding.

Embrace the struggle, embrace the fight,
for in the end, emerges a beacon of light.
A testament to our resilience and might,
a victory born from the depths of our plight.

# Embers of Strength

They say the good die young,
yet so did this —
perhaps it's better than i think it is.

A life extinguished, leaving a void untold.
I trace the outline of your shadow in the hallway,
still warm in memory.
But through the grief and tears, resilience shall rise,
a beacon of strength, beyond earthly demise.

In the face of adversity, we find our might,
even when the night stretches longer than it should.
For in every dark tunnel, there's a glimmer of light.
Though sorrows may haunt and cloud our skies,
resilience guides us, renewing our resolve.

It whispers softly, "*Stand tall and strong;
embrace the challenges, for they won't last long.*"
With determination as our unwavering guide,
we conquer the storms, though our hands shake and hearts ache.

Resilience, the essence of our human spirit,
pushes us forward, reminding us to never quit.
Though life's tests may leave us battered and weary,
we rise again, unyielding and unwary.

When they say the good die young, hold fast this spark.
Resilience ignites hope even from the dark.
With courage to endure and hearts burning bright,
we rise from sorrow and emerge into the light.

# Midnight Domains

In a world where comfort ruled supreme,
we sought a different kind of dream.
While others longed for an easier life,
we forged our path through struggle and strife,
embracing darkness like a midnight call.

Our hometown lay desolate, enclosed by walls.
A wasteland of cages, fences tall,
still, some found solace, achieving it all.
They longed for comfort, a life well-spun,
while we sought battles not yet won.

Some sought support, a life to share,
but we carved our own way, without a care.
Chasing the spotlight, grasping for air,
while others stayed steady, content to remain there.

Through time's deep, reflective glass,
we glimpsed fleeting moments that would forever last.
Unraveling the life we had surpassed,
for them, each day a love that surpassed.

We peered through windows, profound and wide,
witnessing the comfort others had confined.
The life we let slip by, untied,
a silent sacrifice where dreams collide.

They were sunshine, we were rain,
seeking comfort, they avoided pain.
Dreaming of vows, happily ever refrain,
while we carved paths with resilience untamed.

Sometimes we gain what we desire,
yet echoes of the past fuel our inner fire.
They seldom think of us unless we inspire,
and midnight calls, recalling what transpired.

They craved comfort; we embraced pain.
They sought fairy tales; we carved our own domain.
In pursuit of dreams, our ambitions remain,
while others stayed constant, resisting change.

We transformed, as midnight decreed,
yet sometimes we find what we most need.
Haunted by memories, each midnight freed,
a testament to the lives we dared to lead.

# Stronger than Ever

I saw a problem, knew it needed mending,
couldn't ignore the cracks, the breaking, the bending.
I stepped forward, trembling yet determined,
and left my sadness behind, fragmented, unburdened.

Shards of sorrow lay scattered on the floor,
like fragile porcelain, shattered evermore.
Each piece a memory, a hurt I once held tight,
now glimmering in the light, refracted and bright.

I shed the coats of fear and despair,
stripped illusions I no longer wear.
To touch my own skin, raw and real,
to face the quiet core, to finally heal.

Now I rise, taller than before,
each scar a map, a story, a door.
Old keys lie useless, doors left behind,
I move with a strength I once had to find.

It's time to forgive me, who I once blamed,
for choices and chances, for losses unnamed.
I made a change, carved a path of my own,
and now I stand stronger than I've ever known.

Echoes of yesterday still whisper their tune,
yet I dance freely beneath the moon.
No longer haunted by what I cannot reverse,
every step forward is a blessing, not a curse.

This strength is quiet, yet impossible to miss,
a fortress of fragments, my own self-made bliss.
I embrace the storms, the rain, the pain,
for each layer shed has taught what I gain.

Here I am, unbroken, resilient, free,
a testament to the power of becoming me.
And if the world trembles, I will not bend,
for I am stronger now, stronger than ever, my friend.

# Blessings of Resilience

Along life's winding, untamed way,
blessings bloom quietly, often unseen by day.
Their colors deepen in the storms I face,
where trials strip me bare, and I relearn grace.

Through battles fought in silent rooms,
I've learned what truly endures and blooms.
Blessings born through effort and pain
shine the brightest, like light after days of rain.

In the crucible of struggle's fire,
I am molded, burned, yet drawn higher.
Pain becomes teacher, fire becomes guide,
transforming weakness into strength I once tried to hide.

The heart that beats against the odds
knows gratitude, soft and un-applauded.
Triumphs born from adversities faced
carry sweetness no easy joy could replace.

I raise a toast to blessings held dear,
the quiet wins no one else could hear.
Even in darkness, through shadow and strife,
true joy emerges, small, but faithful to life.

With each sunrise, a new chapter starts,
carrying lessons stitched into my heart.
Stronger I stand, though still unsure,
facing tomorrow, fragile – but sure.

As seasons change and time flows on,
my story weaves, my fingerprints drawn.
In life's vast tapestry, frayed and kind,
I leave a legacy of resilience behind.

I move forward with a steady blaze,
ready for what remains or shifts its ways.
In life's wide song, I claim my part,
led by courage, taught by my own heart.

# ACKNOWLEDGMENTS

To those who were there in moments of light and shadow, and to
every reader who carries these words into their own lives —
thank you; you are part of this tapestry.

And, to the unseen threads — the memories, the lessons,
the moments that broke and rebuilt me — I owe you this tapestry.

*With gratitude and light,*

*Ashley M. Stephenson*

# DEAR READER,

Thank you for making the time to read *Tapestry Threads: Life, Death, &*
*Resilience.* May this collection have helped you discover the
interconnectedness of life, death, and resilience, and renewed your
sense of hope and strength.

Life is a tapestry woven with threads of different experiences, both
light and dark. Embrace each moment, for it contributes to the
beauty of the whole picture.

As you continue your journey, may the words from these pages inspire
you to reflect on your own experiences, face challenges with courage,
and embrace change with an open heart. Let resilience be your
guiding light, leading you through the shadows and towards brighter
tomorrows.

Thank you for allowing *Tapestry Threads* to be a part of your story.
I would be grateful if you took a moment to write a short review on
the website where you purchased this book.

Your support means the world to me.

# ABOUT THE AUTHOR

Ashley M. Stephenson is a writer and lifelong seeker of meaning. Drawing on her experience in law, policy, and personal growth, she helps others navigate life's challenges with resilience, clarity, and grace.

Her work has appeared in *Huffington Post*, *Attorney at Law Magazine*, and on multiple national media outlets. Ashley is also the author of *Rise Up: Be Resilient Like You're Running Out of Time*, a book dedicated to inspiring readers to reclaim strength and purpose in every moment.

When she's not writing, Ashley explores the world with her Pug, Loubie, collecting stories, quiet moments, and inspiration for the next journey.

She is also the Founder of **Time to Rise Press, LLC**, a publishing company dedicated to helping writers share their voices with the world.

www.ingramcontent.com/pod-product-compliance
Lightning Source LLC
Chambersburg PA
CBHW032020150726
47990CB00005B/2049